D1197481

ME...
GENEALOGICAL RESEARCH: FOLLOWING
THE PAPER TRAIL TO MEXICO

By: John P. Schmal
and
Donna S. Morales

Heritage Books, Inc.

Published 2002 by

HERITAGE BOOKS, INC.
1540E Pointer Ridge Place
Bowie, Maryland 20716

1-800-398-7709
www.heritagebooks.com

ISBN 0-7884-2139-5

A Complete Catalog Listing Hundreds of Titles
On History, Genealogy, and Americana
Available Free Upon Request

DEDICATION:

Rebecca Alviso

and

Margaret Nevarez

and

Sergio Sosapavon
(1951 – 1986)

Table of Contents

Illustrations

PURPOSE

The purpose of this book is to offer guidelines, suggestions and an outline to help multigenerational Mexican Americans get started with family history research. Utilizing documents from both Mexico and United States, we will show the reader the means by which he or she may be able to procure information from governmental sources or the Family History Library.

Successful Mexican-American genealogical research is actually a series of processes. The first process is the accumulation of information. The numerous processes that follow may involve analysis or document interpretation or just plain searching. If you follow in the footsteps of others and utilize the experience of those who went before you, your work may be simplified.

Mexico probably has the most detailed records in the world, stretching back more than 400 years. Once the reader understands this, he or she will realize that a huge collection of family history information is waiting to be tapped so that Mexican Americans can tell stories about their long fascinating journey through time.

Acknowledgements
by John P. Schmal

I would like to acknowledge the following people and organizations for their contributions, materials and assistance: Professor Julian Nava, Rebecca Alviso, Margaret Nevarez, Jaime Pacheco, the *Kansas City Star*, the Simmons Funeral Home, Carole Turner, Jesse Dominguez, the National Archives Regional Administration, the Immigration and Naturalization Service, the Los Angeles Family History Center, Cambridge University Press, Claire Prechtel-Kluskens, Cyndi Howells, Stefanie Bobar (of the Center for Latin American Studies), Jerry Lubenow (of the Institute of Governmental Studies at Berkeley), Peter Clancey (of the HyperWar Foundation), Diane Edwards (of the University of New Mexico Press), and the Academic Affairs Section of SIL International.

A special thanks goes out to Ms. Loren L. Taylor for allowing us to reproduce a page from *The Ethnic History of Wyandotte County*. An equally special thank you goes to the American Battle Monuments Commission for permitting us to show you the memorial to Donna's uncle, Louis Dominguez (KIA, World War II). Donna and I thank her mother, Ms. Bessie Dominguez Morales, for the beautiful family pictures. Bessie and Daniel Morales are pictured on the cover of this book.

I would like to offer a special thanks to Ms. Kathy Warburton and the Family History Library of Salt Lake City for their permission to reproduce certain documents and for their support of this endeavor. I also offer special thanks to the Genealogical Publishing Company for their permission to reproduce quotations from Dr. George Ryskamp's *Finding Your Hispanic Roots*. Dr. Ryskamp's expertise on this subject provided us with some very profound statements.

Finally, I want to recognize the great contribution that the Catholic Church has made to the documentation and preservation of church records in Mexico for the last 400 years. Their meticulous chronicling of special events in the lifetimes of common Mexican people has made family history research a possibility for all Mexican Americans.

This work has been dedicated to my friends, Rebecca Alviso and Margaret Nevarez. We have also dedicated this book to the memory of my best friend of many years, Sergio Sosapavon. Sergio, who was an educator, came from a family that has dedicated itself to the education of the community. I believe that in some way, our friendship in years past played a role in prompting me to collaborate with Donna in the writing of this book.

PREFACE
by: Professor Julian Nava
Chicano writer, activist and former Ambassador to Mexico

The book by the authors appears at a crossroads in relations between the United States and Mexico. For those that make use of their work the personal direction of their life will surely be affected.

Increasingly the future of both nations is fusing into something new. Economic relations are merging and becoming more interdependent, but so too are the social and cultural life of the two peoples. The United States is Americanizing Mexico and Mexico is Mexicanizing the United States. The Year 2000 Census, on the one hand, and NAFTA on the other, serve as examples of these new conditions.

Over time Mexican Americans have suffered their own forms of prejudice at the hands of other Americans. Although there have been similarities with the prejudice suffered by Indians, Blacks and other minority groups, the Mexican American experience has been shaped by our proximity to Mexico, a war of aggression against Mexico, anti-Catholicism and certain cultural conflicts. Among the defensive reactions used by many, avoiding identification with things Mexican helped the acculturation and assimilation into mainstream America. Such personal casualties claimed to be "Spanish" rather than Mexican.

The chapter on military records is a valuable and surprising component of the book. The material will help with research on the exemplary military service of Mexican Americans. Most folks - including Mexican Americans - do not know that they were the most decorated ethnic group of servicemen in WWII, as well as the Korean and Vietnam conflicts.

Since the "Chicano Era" in the 1960s younger Mexican Americans rejected the hyphenated label and claimed a distinct identity. Today Chicanos, Hispanics and Latinos are terms commonly used as they and others try to define the group.

The authors' work satisfies an emerging thirst among Mexican Americans to search for their roots. More want to understand their roots for personal reasons. It will be a valuable by-product to help them find their place within the context of American life. And, as a result, they will surely see themselves as an asset to American culture and society.

The earlier so-called pioneers journeyed westward, while those from Mexico have journeyed northward. Both traveled at great risk at times, but many Spanish-speaking pioneers had already made the trek northward before Jamestown or Plymouth were settled. Learning about their roots will change the self-image of Americans whose family origins are in Mexico.

The authors provide a great service in this new and popular endeavor. Mexican Americans – a group which is already family-oriented – will be invigorated by learning about the comparatively excellent genealogical records in Mexico. I believe that this handbook will open doors to an edifying past.

INTRODUCTION

Until recently, Mexican-American genealogical research was an under-appreciated and under-utilized art form. However, as the resources and archives of the Family History Library, the Immigration and Naturalization Service, the National Archives and the collections of university libraries become recognized and available to the public, the search for one's Mexican roots has taken a dramatic and fortuitous turn. You – the reader – may be surprised to know that Mexican-American genealogical and family history research can be done without having to visit Mexico.

Suddenly, Mexican Americans in every part of the country are being introduced to resources that will open new doors and permit them to reach two, three or four centuries into the past to locate and study their forebears. But, the most important resource in Mexican-American research is "you."

You – the Mexican-American student, teacher, doctor, soldier, librarian, mother, father, mechanic, or grandparent – can learn the simple steps required to initiate a successful search into your family's history. Our book has been designed for you – the English-speaking Mexican-American whose family has been in America for more than two generations. We designed it with your questions in mind and we attempt, in the following pages, to answer some of those questions. In addition, we make suggestions that may help you obtain important and crucial information for your research.

The most important piece of information for you to obtain is the name of the place from which your Mexican ancestors came. In this respect, your dilemma is the same as every other ethnic group that came to America. If you cannot locate your ancestral town, it will be very difficult for you to get past the border to research your family's history in Mexico.

A multitude of resources may help you figure out the name of that ancestral town or village. Naturalization papers, alien registration forms, border-crossing documents, death certificates, obituaries and mortuary records all have potential value in locating crucial information. And this information will be at your fingertips if you know how to locate it.

For the person born in Mexico, our guide can be equally useful. In the second half of the book, we present documents that illustrate the wonderful detail found in many Mexican church and civil records. In addition, we discuss the problems associated with racial classifications found in most Mexican documents before 1822 (independence). As an added dimension to Mexican ancestral research, we discuss the *Catalogo de Pasajeros a Indias* series, which give the names of many Spanish immigrants who immigrated from Spain to the Western Hemisphere during the Sixteenth Century.

If your ancestors came from Mexico, you are very lucky. The records that Mexico has maintained over the last 400 years are far superior to those from most other countries. We hope that you will be able to utilize our suggestions so that you can follow your own paper trail to Mexico.

Chapter One
Following the Paper Trail
Donna Morales

My name is Donna Morales and I am a Mexican-American woman from Kansas City. Although I was born and raised in Kansas City, I have also lived in Houston, Texas and Los Angeles, California. In 2000, I collaborated with my friend, John Schmal, in putting together an unpublished work entitled *My Family Through Time: The Story of a Mexican-American Family.*[1]

John has been specializing in Mexican research for over a decade and he did most of the Mexican genealogical research for our book. Our book has traced some portions of my family back 400 years to Aguascalientes and across the Atlantic Ocean to Pamplona (in the Basque country of northern Spain) and Triana (near Sevilla in southern Spain). Later in this book, you, the reader, will see selected documents of my ancestors from *My Family Through Time.*

We have put together this presentation as a guide to help multi-generational Mexican Americans locate where in Mexico their ancestors came from. Dr. George Ryskamp, in his book, *Finding Your Hispanic Roots*, writes the following passage about Hispanic genealogical research:[2]

> [An] exciting fact about doing Hispanic family history research is that chances for success are better in Spain and her former colonies than anywhere else in the world... In Hispanic countries most families can trace their ancestry into the seventeenth century...

For the great detail that is to be found in Mexican records, we can thank the Catholic Church. At the Council of Trent (1545-1563), the Catholic authorities required that each of the Catholic parishes would keep records

---

[1] Donna S. Morales and John P. Schmal, *My Family Through Time: The Story of a Mexican-American Family* (2000).

[2] George R. Ryskamp, *Finding Your Hispanic Roots* (Baltimore: Genealogical Publishing Co., Inc., 1997), p. 3.

of baptisms, marriages and deaths. Continuing with this thought, Dr. Ryskamp explains that:[3]

> Truly it can be said that Catholicism has contributed more to the shaping of Hispanic life and society than any single factor... Hispanic parishes were not only the principal units of ecclesiastical organization but also the main social unit for much of the rural life in Hispanic countries. Because of the intimate daily role the parish played and in many areas still plays, its registers usually provide the most extensive and accurate glimpse into the lives of your Spanish ancestors. For centuries the registers of Hispanic parishes have documented the lives of even the poorest laborers in tiny villages throughout Spain and Latin America.

Over the years, the Family History Library of Salt Lake City has acquired the microfilmed records of churches and civil archives throughout Mexico. As a matter of fact, 150,000 rolls of microfilm are now available for in-library viewing and analysis at the main library in Salt Lake or at any of the associated 1,400 Family History Centers found throughout the United States. If you would like to check the holdings of the library, you can access the Family History Library Catalog on the internet at the following URL: *http://www.familysearch.org/Eng/Library/FHLC/frameset_fhlc.asp*. If you want to locate the availability of records for a given city in Mexico, just enter the name of the city in the ***Place Search*** field.

The availability of these records is a great help for people seeking to trace their Mexican ancestry. However, for people whose ancestors came from Mexico during the Revolution (1910-1920) or in the subsequent period, it is possible that you are not aware of exactly where your ancestors came from. And, in order to begin tracing your family tree, you need to locate a place of origin. The following pages will help you – the reader – to understand the many options available to you in your research.

---

[3] *Ibid.*, p. 157.

Chapter 2
Finding Vital Records
John P. Schmal

Dr. Ryskamp has referred to vital records as "government or church records of major life events such as births or baptisms, marriages, and deaths."[1] Vital records of your ancestors can be crucial tools in locating your immigrant ancestors because they will probably give you information that you might have been unaware of. Every death, marriage, or birth record is like a piece of one gigantic puzzle, telling a small but significant part of your family's history. If you collect as many of these vital records as possible, a clearer picture of your family's past will emerge.

To illustrate my point, on page 4, you will see the Kansas birth certificate for one Roman Juarez, who was born on August 9, 1919 in Montgomery County, Kansas. Please note that this document lists the parents of Roman, their ages, and the name of the state in Mexico from which they came (Chihuahua).

Death certificates can be as important to your research as birth records. On page 5, we have reproduced the 1941 death certificate of Modesta Silva Elizalde. Modesta died in Los Angeles and, as you can see, relevant information about her death is given. In addition, Modesta's date of birth (June 24, 1877) is provided, along with her birthplace (Tularosa, New Mexico). What is most interesting about this document is the fact that both her parents' names are listed, and the state of Zacatecas (in Mexico) has been given as their place of birth. One occasional problem with death records is that the information is given by the next-of-kin and it is possible that the grieving relative may have given erroneous information. So, while we assume that a death certificate is telling the truth, we must understand that some inaccurate information may be present in the document.

---

[1] *Ibid.*, p. 11.

Birth Certificate of Roman Juarez

1941 Death Certificate of Modesta Silva Elizalde

On page 7, we have reproduced the 1937 marriage record of Antonio Elizalde and Nicolasa Garcia. Antonio was the son of Sotero Elizalde and Modesta Silva (the subject of the previous document). As you can see, the marriage record is very specific about the origins of Antonio's parents, but not about the parents of Nicolasa Garcia. All we learn of Nicolasa is that she and her parents were born somewhere in Mexico.

Locating vital records for your ancestor may answer some important questions and help point you in the right direction. Several websites have been designed to help you locate vital records information for various states. Cyndi Howells has designed a series of websites, known as "Cyndi's List of Genealogy Sites on the Internet," each of which link to multiple sites on a given topic. Among her many useful sites, you will find "U.S. – Vital Records: Birth, Marriage, Divorce and Death," located at *http://www.cyndislist.com/usvital.htm.* This website is an excellent place to start.

We also recommend the website, entitled "Vital Records Information – United States. This URL, located at *http://vitalrec.com/,* allows you to link to your state of choice. In some cases, an individual website may lead you to birth or death indexes for a given state. For example, if you are looking for California deaths from 1940 to 1997, you can do a search in the 500,000-name database at:
http://userdb.rootsweb.com/ca/death/search.cgi.

People trying to find out information on writing for Texas vital records can access the following URL: *http://vitalrec.com/tx.html.* This website has links to indexes that may prove useful for your search.

One of the best websites, located at: *http://home.att.net/~wee-monster/deathrecords.html*, is entitled "Online Searchable Death Indexes for the USA: A Guide for Genealogists and Other Researchers." This URL probably offers more links to state vital records indexes than any other website.

In conclusion, acquiring vital records should serve as one of the first steps in your family history research. Birth, death and marriage records frequently open the door to other options.

1937 Marriage Record of Antonio Elizalde & Nicolasas Garcia

Chapter 3
Other Sources of Vital Information
Donna Morales

Vital records will play an important role in researching your family history. As a matter of fact, they usually open the door to finding other sources of vital information that may help you to investigate your family. These other sources include census schedules, church records, cemetery inscriptions, social security records, and obituaries. All these collateral sources of information may go a long way in helping you to reconstruct the history of your family.

If your ancestors came to America during the Mexican Revolution (1910-1920) or earlier, American census records can be invaluable sources of information and may be able help you trace the patterns of your family's movement. If you believe that your family moved around – as did migrant laborers and some railroad workers – the census may be able to pinpoint their location in a particular place at a given time.

However, census-takers often misspelled names, especially when they interviewed immigrants who spoke with a heavy accent or in a foreign tongue. To help get around this problem, the Census Bureau created a tool that is commonly referred to as the soundex.

The soundex is a coded surname index based on the sound. This form of indexing groups together similar-sounding surnames into one code. The soundex coding system was developed to enable researchers to search for a given surname under several different spellings. Thus, a given soundex code may include several surnames. Each soundex code consists of a letter and three numbers. The first letter of the surname as seen on the census is the letter at the beginning of the code.

The following codes are assigned to the indicated letters:

Code	Letters
1	b, p, f, v
2	c, s, k, g, j, q, x, z
3	d, t
4	l
5	m, n
6	r

The letters a, e, i, o, u, y, w, and h are not coded at all. Using this system, the surname Rodriguez would receive the following soundex code: R-362. The soundex code for my maternal ancestors, Dominguez, is D-552, while my father's Morales ancestors were located under the soundex code M-642.

As an example of how the soundex can help you locate your ancestors, we have reproduced several examples of census information. In our research, we looked for a Pabla Martinez in the 1920 census. We only knew that Pabla had been born around the turn of the century in Webb County, Texas, and that her parents names were Felipe and Maria Luisa Martinez.

On page 11 is the 1920 soundex card for the family of Felipe and Luisa Martinez. Some of the categories found in the soundex cards are abbreviated and knowing these abbreviations is a key to understanding the data presented. At the top of the card, Felipe Martinez – as the head of this household – is described as "W" (White), 47 years old, born in Mexico, and living in Webb County. Under citizenship, we can see the designation "1888 Al." In this category for foreign-born heads of families, you may find the following abbreviations: "Al" for Alien, "Pa" for "first papers" (for citizenship), and "Na" for naturalized citizen. In this case, Felipe is classified as an alien and states that he arrived in the United States in 1888.

Under "Other Members of the Family," we can see the names of his wife and children. Luisa is listed as "W" (Wife), 37 years of age, and a native of Texas. The relationship to the head of the household, age and birthplace of each child is also listed: Paubla (who is 20 years old), Elutiria, Tawesa, and Maximiano. On the top of the second card were will find Aurora, Eloisa, and Romana. It is worth noting that first names are even more likely to be misspelled than surnames. It is possible that Elutiria may actually be spelled Eleuteria, while Tawesa may actually be Theresa.

In the right-hand corner of the top of the soundex card we see several numbers. The most important number here is the one in the E.D. (Enumeration District) category. The entire census and each city or county is divided into enumeration districts. In this case, in order to find

M635

Martinez, Felipe
(HEAD OF FAMILY)

STATE **TEXAS**

VOL. *169* E.D. *184*

SHEET *3* LINE *18*

W	47	Mexico	1888 al
(COLOR)	(AGE)	(BIRTHPLACE)	(CITIZENSHIP)

Webb
(COUNTY)

(CITY)	(STREET)	(HOUSE NO.)

OTHER MEMBERS OF FAMILY

NAME	RELATION-SHIP	AGE	BIRTHPLACE	CITIZEN-SHIP
Martinez, Luisa	W	37	Texas	
— Paula	D	20	Texas	
— Elutiria	D	18	Texas	
— Tomesa	D	16	Texas	
— Maximiano	S	13	Texas	

1920 CENSUS—INDEX
DEPARTMENT OF COMMERCE # 1 see # 2
BUREAU OF THE CENSUS

A-16

U. S. GOVERNMENT PRINTING OFFICE

Martinez, Felipe
(HEAD OF FAMILY—CONTINUED)

STATE Texas

OTHER MEMBERS OF FAMILY—CONTINUED

NAME	RELATION-SHIP	AGE	BIRTHPLACE	CITIZEN-SHIP
Martinez, Aurora	D	7	Texas	
— Eloisa	D	4 3/12	Texas	
— Romana	D	4/12	Texas	

1920 Census Soundex-Household of Felipe Martinez

the individual listing of the head of household (Felipe Martinez), we will look for the microfilm reel that includes Webb County, Enumeration District 184, on Sheet (page) 3, and at Line 18. The rest of the family members will be listed in the subsequent rows.

The National Archives has a website dedicated primarily to helping an individual understand and use the soundex code. This website, entitled "The Soundex Indexing System," can be accessed at :
http://www.archives.gov/research_room/genealogy/census/soundex.htm l. It is obvious that the soundex card alone can provide you with very important information on your ancestors. But the soundex has been designed to lead you to the actual census schedules where more information can be found.

On page 13, we have reproduced part of the 1920 census reading for the family of Felipe Martinez. At the top of the page, we are given information relating to the location of this household. The family of Felipe lives in Justice Precinct #2 of the county of Webb in the state of Texas. The Enumeration District and Page Number for this sheet – always located in the far right corner at the top of the page – is not visible on this reproduction.

Five different families and households are shown here before we come to Felipe Martinez, who is listed as living on a "Fm" (Farm) at Dwelling 41. If you note the descriptions at the top of each column, you will be able to decipher the meaning of each category. The first four columns all relate to "Place of Adobe": Address, Dwelling Number and Family Number. Then, as you read across the row from left to right, you will find that Felipe Martinez was the head of the household, and "R" (rented) his home.

Under the four columns relating to "Personal Description," you will see that Felipe was described as a "M" (Male), "W" (White), 47 years of age, and married. Under the "Citizenship" column, we can see that Felipe arrived in the U.S. in 1888 and was classified as an alien. The columns describing "Education," "Nativity and Mother Tongue," and "Occupation" that follow, can also be very informative.

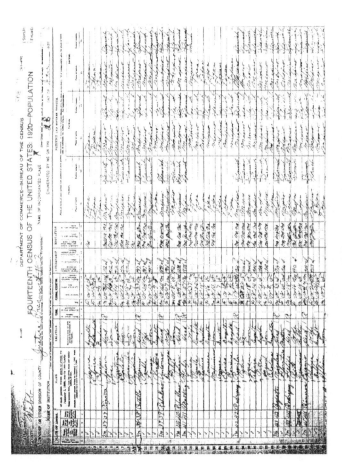

1920 Census Schedules–Household of Felipe Martinez

Under the first column in "Nativity and Mother Tongue," we can see that Felipe was born in Mexico and that his mother tongue was Spanish. The same information is also given for both his father and mother. From the 1880 census to the 1930 census, the schedules have provided this information about each person's parentage. The column listing "Occupation" – appearing at the far-right hand corner of the sheet – is not visible on this reproduction.

Looking at the row that follows Felipe Martinez' information, we see his wife Luisa listed. Luisa was tallied as a "F" (Female), "W" (White), 37 years old, and "M" (Married). Because she was born in the United States, there is no information to be found in the "Citizenship" columns. Luisa stated that she was born in Texas and it is assumed that she probably speaks "English" because the column for "Mother Tongue" was left blank. However, we do find out that both of her parents were born in Mexico and that their mother-tongues were Spanish.

The information for Paubla and her siblings is also provided. Scanning down the row on the information listed for Paubla, we can see that she was the daughter of the head of household (Felipe), "F" (Female), "W" (White), 20 years old, and "S" (Single). Paubla was born in Texas, but under the nativity of father, we can see that her father (Felipe) was born in Mexico. Under the nativity of mother, Luisa is described as a native of Texas.

If it is very clear from the information provided by the 1920 census that your ancestors were also living in the United States during 1900 or 1910, it is likely that you will want to do follow up research by checking those census schedules. Only twenty-one of the states have been soundexed for the 1910 census. Texas, California, Illinois, and Kansas – states that many Mexican immigrants traveled to – are soundexed for this year. Arizona and New Mexico, unfortunately, were not soundexed.

But all the states are soundexed for the 1900 census and our next step was to try and find the young family of Felipe Martinez in this census. We were not sure whether Felipe lived in Webb County or some other part of Texas because it was believed he might have been a migrant worker who moved around for a few years. But we knew that the soundex would track him down and so we turned to the 1900 soundex for some answers.

The 1900 soundex card reproduced on page 16 lists the household of one Felipe Martinez. The fact that this card refers to the 1900 census is indicated at the lower left-hand corner. In this census, we can see that Felipe Martinez has been classified as "W" (White), was born in August of 1873, and was 26 years old in Mexico. He lives in Precinct 4 of Webb County, Texas and apparently had filed his "first papers" for citizenship.

Also listed in this household is Felipe's wife Luisa Martinez, who was born in August 1881, was 18 years old, and a native of Texas. The first of their children, Paula Martinez, was also listed as a "D" (Daughter). Her month and year of birth are listed as March 1899 and she was one year of age at the time of the census. At the top left-hand corner, we can see that the head of this household will be found in Enumeration District 96 (of Webb County), Sheet (Page) 12, and Line 21.

Utilizing the information learned from the soundex card, we then decided to move on to the actual census schedules for the 1900 census. The 1900 census listing for Felipe Martinez, reproduced on page 17, indicates that Felipe Martinez was the head of household in Dwelling 225 and Household 225.

But the most important information we found was not under Felipe's column. We noticed that Martinez was not spelled out as Felipe's surname. Instead, he was listed with several Martinez individuals spread across two households. Living in the first household (Dwelling 224) was Maximiano Martinez, a native of Mexico.

One of the most important aspects of census research is that additional clues to your ancestry may be found in the same neighborhood as the family you are studying. In this case, the proximity of Maximiano and Paula Martinez leads us to believe that there is probably a familial relationship between the two families.

While it is possible that Maximiano Martinez may be a much older brother or an uncle of Felipe Martinez, it is more likely that 26-year-old Felipe is the son of 50-year-old Maximiano and 46-year-old Paula. It is worth nothing that in the 1920 census, Felipe and Maximiano Martinez household's 1920 census, Felipe and Luisa had a son named Maximiano.

1900 Census Soundex-Household of Felipe Martinez

1900 Census Schedules-Felipe Martinez

17

We may infer that the son Maximiano might have been named for his grandfather, Maximiano Martinez. We may also infer that the children of Maximiano and Luisa Martinez are probably younger siblings of Felipe still living at home.

Under the column of Maximiano Martinez, we find that he is listed as the head of household, "W" (White), "M" (Male), was born in January of 1850, and was 50 years old. His marital status was "M" (Married) and he had been married for a total of 28 years at the time the census was taken. Maximiano is listed as having been born in Mexico, similar to both his parents. Under the next columns relating to citizenship, he also states that he arrived in the U.S. in 1876, thirty-four years earlier. "Pa" indicates that he had filed for "first papers" for citizenship.

Paula Martinez, the wife of Maximiano, is listed as the "Wife" of the head of household, "W" (White), "F" (Female), born in February 1854. She was 46 years of age and had been married for 28 years. In the column after marriage status, the numbers "8" and "6" mean that Paula had given birth to eight children, of which six were still living at the time of the census. Paula was also born in Mexico and arrived in the U.S. in 1876. Five children were listed as living at home with the parents.

Moving down to the household of Felipe Martinez, apparently next door, Felipe Martinez is listed as "W" (White), "M" (Male) and had been born in August 1873. He was 26 years of age, and stated that he had been married for three years to his wife. His birthplace is also given as Mexico and he apparently accompanied his parents to the United States in 1876.

Luisa is listed as the "Wife" of the Head of Household, "W" (White), "F" (Female) and born in August 1881. She was 18 years old and had already been married for three years. Under the next two columns, we learn that Luisa had given birth to one child and that one child was still living. In the next row, their first-born child Paula was also listed.

The enormous information that may be provided by locating your ancestors in the 1900, 1910, and 1920 censuses can be a great help aid. Because the census finds a family and pins them down to a given location at a given time, it is then possible for you to locate other records.

Using the Family History Library Catalog or local city directories, it is likely that you can find if further information may be located in church or county records.

It is possible for you to search the census soundex and census schedules at Family History Centers, National Archives facilities, and at some public libraries. You can also order census microfilm via interlibrary loan and use this wonderful resource at your library of choice. Several National Archives sites may be helpful in getting you started. A good place to begin would be NARA's "Clues in Census Records, 1850-1930," located at the following URL: *http://www.archives.gov/research_room/genealogy/census/census_clues_1850_to_1930.html.* Another NARA website, "How to Use NARA's Census Microfilm Catalog," can provide useful clues to working with each census year. This URL is located at: *http://www.archives.gov/research_room/genealogy/census/using_census_microfilm_catalogs.html.* Other Internet sites discussing census research are:

1. *http://www.hpl.lib.tx.us/clayton/soundex.html*
2. *http://freepages.education.rootsweb.com/~mdtmgug/census.htm*
3. *http://www.colorado.edu/libraries/govpubs/debbie/soundx.htm*

Another source of vital information may be the newspaper obituary. On page 20, we have reproduced the obituary and memorial for my father, Daniel Morales. The obituary, published in the *Kansas City Star* following my father's death on November 16, 1996, pays tribute to my father's numerous contributions of the Kansas City community.

On page 21, we have reproduced the obituary of my first cousin, Eleno D. Salazar, Jr., who died in 1988. As you can see, this obituary pays tribute to Cousin Eleno's service in the Korean War and tells us about his occupation. Not all obituaries are as detailed as these two examples, but many can offer useful clues for your research.

In many parts of this country, county historical and genealogical societies publish county history books. Sometimes these books pay tribute to certain members of the community, perhaps with a biographical paragraph or two. As a matter of fact, entire books are sometimes dedicated to cemetery inscriptions, church baptisms and old census records.

--DANIEL S. MORALES

Daniel S. Morales, 82, Mission, KS, passed away November 16, 1996, at Trinity Lutheran Manor. Funeral services 10 a.m. Tuesday, November 19, at Simmons Funeral Home; burial in Maple Hill Cemetery. Friends may call 4-7 p.m. Monday, November 18, at Simmons Funeral Home. The family suggests memorial contributions be made to Kansas City Hospice.

Mr. Morales was born September 23, 1914, in Houston, TX, and had been a resident of the Kansas City area since 1932. He was a clerk for the Rock Island Railroad, retiring in 1975, after 38 years of service. He was a Sunday school teacher for over 40 years at the First Spanish American Baptist Church of Kansas City, KS, and was a Scout Master for Troop #230 for 17 years. Survivors include his wife, Bessie Paula (Dominguez) Morales, of the home; eight daughters, Jenny Hobeck, Los Angeles, CA, Olivia Tilden, Olathe, KS, Mary Ellen Day, Prairie Village, KS, Eleanor Clark and Ruth Williams, both of Kansas City, KS, Carol Patterson, Jefferson City, MO, Donna Crawford, Houston, TX, and Abigail Garcia, Blue Springs, MO; a sister, Carmen Dominguez, Kansas City, KS; 16 grandchildren; and 16 great-grandchildren. The family is grateful to Kansas City Hospice and his nurse, Duane Carlson.

2007 ———— IN MEMORIAM

In Loving Memory of
DANIEL MORALES

September 23, 1913 November 16, 1996

It broke our hearts to lose you, but you did not go alone, For part of us went with you, the day GOD called you home. "Dad you are still our Hero!!!" We were blessed to have you. Wife: Bessie, daughters: Juanita, Olivia, Mary Ellen, Eleanor, Carol, Donna, Ruth and Abigale, Grandchildren and Great-Grandchildren.

Obituary of Daniel Morales

ELENO D. SALAZAR JR.

Eleno D. Salazar Jr., 57, Kansas City, Kan., died Feb. 21, 1988, at Bethany Medical Center. He was born in Lyman, Neb., and lived in Kansas City, Kan., most of his life. Mr. Salazar worked for the Santa Fe Railway and later was an upholsterer. He was an Air Force veteran of the Korean War. Survivors include three sons, Eleno D. Salazar III and Jesse Heineken of Kansas City, Kan., and Mike Salazar, Mission; his mother, Julia D. Salazar, Kansas City, Kan.; three brothers, Martin Salazar, Kansas City, Kan., John Salazar, Independence, and Jerry Salazar, Olathe; and four grandchildren. Services will be at 1 p.m. Wednesday at the Spanish Nazarene Church; burial in Maple Hill Cemetery. Friends may call from 5 to 9 p.m. today at the Simmons Chapel, where devotional services will be at 7 p.m.

Obituary of Eleno Salazar, Jr.

For example, Ms. Loren L. Taylor, in her 1992 publication *The Ethnic History of Wyandotte County*, discussed the Mexican-American community of Kansas City. On page 23, we have reproduced one page from that book, listing the baptism records of Mexican-American children at St. Bridget's Catholic Church. Each entry gives the name of the child, the baptism date, and the names of the parents and godparents. There are several pages of these entries and, for the person whose Mexican-American roots are in Kansas City; these entries may prove to be very useful.[1]

Finally, two very important sources of information are mortuary or funeral home records. Some mortuaries keep records that are even more detailed than the county death certificates. But, the accessibility of mortuary records varies from one place to the next. Sometimes, a mortuary may destroy some of its records after a certain period of time has passed.

But, in other areas, the funeral records may stretch back more than fifty or sixty years. If the death was fairly recent, it is likely that the mortuary will probably only release the records to a relative or direct descendant of the decedent.

On page 24, we have reproduced the 1990 Record of Funeral for my Uncle Celestino Morales. John sent for this record several years ago and, as you can see, it gives us a fair amount of information. As it turns out, this date of birth (April 8, 1908) was correct and we used this information to find Uncle Celestino's baptism and civil birth records in Aguascalientes, Mexico. This document eventually helped us to trace my Morales ancestors and their collateral lines back almost 400 years.

On page 25, we have reproduced the Record of Funeral for my Aunt Julia's husband, Eleno H. Salazar, who died in October 1968. This record gives the names of Eleno's parents and his date of birth as August 18, 1908 (in Mexico). Most valuable of all, the names of Eleno's parents give us some clues about the next generation. As you can see by the cited records, the Record of Funeral can be a useful tool for obtaining information about a deceased relative.

---

[1] Loren L. Taylor, *The Ethnic History of Wyandotte County* (Kansas City, Kansas: Kansas Ethnic Council, 1992).

At that time there was no Mexican Parish in which the incoming Mexican families could express their proud culture. This was in marked contrast to Armourdale where the incoming Mexican families were treated with less than acceptance into the St. Thomas Parish. It appears that there may well have been Mexican families in Armourdale that traveled to St. Bridget Parish, during this period, to have their children baptized in the growing Mexican community and the more culturally friendly environment. The Mexican parish of St. John Mt. St. Carmel in Armourdale was not created until 1923. St. John The Divine in Argentine was not created until 1937.

The few remaining records from St. Bridget Parish showed that the first Mexican American child to be baptized was **John Manriquez** who was born on June 12, 1910 to **Jacinto Mariquez** and **Laurencia (Ruiz) Manriquez**. He was baptized on June 19, 1910 with **Paulino Manriquez** and **Anna Kenan** as godparents. He later married **Lois Sue James** at Holy Name Church in Kansas City, Kansas. The second child was **Emmanuel Lopez** who was baptized on January 22, 1911. He was the son of **Bentura Lopez** and **Julia (Jantcella) Lopez**. His godparents were **Jacinto Manriquez** and **Florencia Ruiz**. The third was **Jesus Joannes Adriano** who was born on November 29, 1910 to **Mathias Adriano** and **Philippa (Diaz) Adrino**. He was baptized on August 13, 1911 with **Conception Navarro** and **Emiteria Moreno** as godparents.

The following baptisms were recorded in the Parish records:

Name	Baptized	Parents	Godparents
Felix Candeleg	2-4-1912 Born 1-14-1912	Catherino Candeleg Juana Arsenjura	Israel Soria Guadalupe Bautista
Maria Jalindo	2-4-1912 Born 12-7-1910	Mr. & Mrs. Paulus Jalindo	Manuel Rodelo Elidia Romero
Joseph Manriquez	5-9-1912 5-9-1912	Jacinto Manriquez Florentia Ruiz	Manuel & Elidia Rodelo
Theodorus Rodelo	5-26-1912 B-5-26-12	Manuel Rodelo Elidia Romero	Roseleo Basquez Josephine Manriquez
Juanita De la Torre	6-30-1912 6-25-12	Jesus Maria De la Torre Petra De la Torre	Luz Ernandez Polonia & De la Torre
Maria Sandoval	3-28-1914 3-21-1914	Frank Sandoval Josepha Martinez	John Gomez Midela Gomez
Margarita Mondivque	4-3-1914 3-31-1914	Jacinto Mondivque Florentia Rios	Michael Barrett Catherine Barrett
Josephine Montes	11-4-1916 10-10-16	Jose' Montes Maria Ramierez	Francisco Sandoval Juana Padilla
Joseph Mondirgue	9-22-1917 9-22-1917	James Mondirgue Florence Rios	Mary Brasckenve ldt
Maria de Socurso Mondirque	9-22-1917 9-22-1917	James Mondirque Florence Rio	M Gulielmus Brasckenve ldt
Ereverto Mansacvo	2-17-1918 12-20-17	Peter Mansalvo Mary Ontiveros	Melchior Martinez
Petrus M. Alcantara	4-14-1918 3-6-1918	Marcellinus Alcantara Rosa Selio	Petrus & Maria Ivarra
Cira Felix	5-5-1918 2-24-1918	Henricus Felix Rebecca Olivo	Frances & Petra Garcia

Page from *The Ethnic History of Wyandotte County*

RECORD OF FUNERAL

Permit No. .... Local No. **72** .... Yearly No. **4** .... No .... Date of Entry **July 16, 90**

NAME OF DECEASED **Celestino** Maiden name **MORALES** (aka)

So. Sec. No. .... Sex. **M.** Married .... Never Married .... Widowed .... Other ....

Color or Race **White** .... Origin ....

GENERAL INFORMATION

Address **2837 Bellview**

Kansas City, Missouri

Family Name **567-6350**

Date of Birth **April 4, 1908** Age **82 yrs**

Birthplace **Aguas Calientes, Mexico**

Occupation **Serviced PRESSES for**

Industry or Business **NAZARENE PUBLISHING HOUSE**

Survivors **Sons & DAUGHTERS**

Name of Spouse ....

Maiden Name ....

Name of Father **Eulalio Morales**

Name of Mother **Juanita Martinez**

Maiden Name ....

If Veteran ....

Dates of Service **No**

Serial No. ....

Rank .... Branch ....

Place of Entry/Discharge .... Claim No. ....

Type of Separation ....

Citizenship **USA**

Date of Death **July 14, 1990**

Date of Funeral **July 20, 1990** Time **1:00 am**

Services at **SPANISH CHURCH OF NAZARENE**

Clergyman **Jose Carillo**

Religion of Deceased ....

Resided in the State **Most of life**

Place of Death **DON TRUMAN MED CENTER Mo**

Cause of Death **Atherosclerotic**

Contributory Causes **Heart Disease**

Certifying Physician **Dr. John Ockerman**

City **KC MO** Phone .... or coroner

Ship Remains to ....

CEMETERY or CREMATORY **Maple Hill**

Address **K.C.K.**

Lot No. ....

Grave No. ....

Section No. ....

Block No. ....

Owner ....

Sketch of Lot or Vault ....

Date of Internment **July 20, 1990**

OBITUARY NOTICE

[obituary text obscured]

CHARGES
Complete Funeral ....

SERVICES
Services of Director and Staff ....
Viewing/Visitation ....
Funeral/Memorial Service ....
Graveside/Committal Service ....
Escort ....
Embalming **Corey Senna** ....
Dressing Body **✓** + cosmetology ....
Hairdresser/Cosmetician ....
Autopsy Repair ....

Moving Remains to Funeral Home **Hickey**
Direct Cremations ....
Immediate Burials ....

TOTAL ....

ARRANGEMENTS/FACILITIES
Transfer of Remains ....
Use of Preparation Room ....
Use of Holding Room **Rose Wedge**
Use of Refrigeration ....
Use of Facilities for Viewing ....
Large/Small Room ....
Use of Facilities for Ceremony ....
Large/Small Room ....

Motor Vehicles
Utility Car (first-call) **physicians cas.**
Hearse ....
Limousines **(1) Family car**
Flower Car ....

Outlay for Lot ....
Opening of Grave of Vault ....
Clergy .... Church ....
Singer .... Organist ....
Package Cost ....

TOTAL ....

MERCHANDISING
Register Book ....
Acknowledgement Cards ....
Memorial Cards **1 Box**
Suit or Dress ....
Burial Vault **KL Vault**

Cash Advances
Death Certificate ....
Obituary and Death Notices ....
Permit ....
Liner/Vault ....
Flowers ....
Crucifix/Cross ....
Rosary Beads ....
Pallbearers ....
Common carrier for shipping ....
Telephone/Telegraph ....

TOTAL ....

CASKET or CONTAINER
Mfr. **Art Co** Model .... Type ....
Interior **1400 Gray** .... Color ....
Finish .... Style ....
Exterior **Cloth** .... Color ....
Nameplate ....
Casket Price ....
Alternative Container ....
Outer Receptacle ....

1990 Record of Funeral for Celestino Morales

1968 Record of Funeral for Eleno H. Salazar

Chapter 4
Naturalization Records
John Schmal

The United States is a nation of immigrants. For the family history researcher, the move from a foreign nation to America represents an important phase in each family story. In many cases, the new Americans forgot about their roots while trying to assimilate into American society. Although the details of your family's origin in the "Mother Country" may be lost with the passage of time, naturalization records may be your most valuable tools in locating a place of origin for your immigrant ancestors from Mexico.

As a general rule, naturalization was a two-step process that took a minimum of five years. After residing in the United States for two years, an alien resident could file a *Declaration of Intent* (also referred to as the *First Papers*) at a local court and declare that he intended to become an American citizen. This was the first step in the naturalization process.

After three additional years, the alien, having fulfilled the residency requirements for citizenship, could return to the court and submit a *Petition for Naturalization* (also known as *Second Papers* or *Final Papers*). After the petition was granted, a certificate of citizenship was issued to the person.

On page 28 we have reproduced the September 29, 1941 *Declaration of Intention* for Reynalda Martinez. You can see that this document is very detailed. Among other things, the declaration gives Reynalda's date of birth, birthplace, date and port of arrival, name of spouse, marriage date and place, physical description, and place of residence. According to her own account, Reynalda had immigrated to America from Mexico twenty-nine years earlier.[1]

---

[1] The naturalization documents for Reynalda Martinez have been made available through the courtesy of Margaret Nevarez.

DUPLICATE
(To accompany
monthly report on
Form N-4)

UNITED STATES OF AMERICA

DECLARATION OF INTENTION No.

(Invalid for all purposes seven years after the date hereof)

In the **DISTRICT**

UNITED STATES OF AMERICA | ss | ONE UNITED STATES of LOS ANGELES
SOUTHERN DISTRICT OF CALIFORNIA |

(1) My full, true, and correct name is REYNOLDA MARTINEZ

(2) My present place of residence is 156 No. Hicks, L. A. Cal. (3) My occupation is housewife

(4) I am 49 years old. (5) I was born on Aug 29, 1892 in Tepehuanzo, Mex.

(6) My personal description is as follows: Sex female, color white, complexion med., color of eyes brown,
color of hair brn, height 5 feet 1 inches, weight 124 pounds, visible distinctive marks none,
race Spanish, present nationality Mexican

(7) I am married, the name of my wife or husband is Jose, we were married 10-7-22
at Santa Ana, Cal. he or she was born at Mexico City Mex.
on Not known and entered the United States at El Paso, Tex.
on 1908 for permanent residence in the United States, and now resides with me.

(8) I have one child, and the name, sex, date and place of birth, and present place of residence of each of said children who is living, are as follows:
Jose m 1-7-12 with me born in Tepehuano, Mex.

(9) My last place of foreign residence was Juarez, Mex. (10) I emigrated to the United States from
Same

(11) My lawful entry for permanent residence in the United States was at
El Paso, Tex. (Reynalda Nevarez) under the name of April 15, 1912
on April 15, 1912 on the

(12) Since my lawful entry for permanent residence I have not been absent from the United States, for a period or periods of 6 months or longer, as follows:

DEPARTED FROM THE UNITED STATES				RETURNED TO THE UNITED STATES		
PORT	DATE (Month, day, year)	VESSEL OR OTHER MEANS OF CONVEYANCE		PORT	DATE (Month, day, year)	VESSEL OR OTHER MEANS OF CONVEYANCE

(13) I have not heretofore made a declaration of intention: No. on in the at

(14) It is my intention in good faith to become a citizen of the United States and to reside permanently therein. (15) I will, before being admitted to citizenship, renounce absolutely and forever all allegiance and fidelity to any foreign prince, potentate, state, or sovereignty of whom or which at the time of admission to citizenship I may be a subject or citizen. (16) I am not an anarchist; nor a believer in the unlawful damage, injury, or destruction of property, or sabotage; nor a disbeliever in or opposed to organized government; nor a member of or affiliated with any organization or body of persons teaching disbelief in or opposition to organized government. (17) I certify that the photograph affixed to the duplicate and triplicate hereof is a likeness of me and was signed by me.
I do swear (affirm) that the statements I have made and the intentions I have expressed in this declaration of intention subscribed by me are true to the best of my knowledge and belief; SO HELP ME GOD.

Reynalda Martinez

Subscribed and sworn to (affirmed) before me in the form of oath shown above in the office of the
Clerk of said Court, Los Angeles, Cal.
this 29th day of Sept. Anno Domini 41. I hereby certify that
Certification No. 25 R 163990 from the Commissioner of Immigration and Naturalization showing the lawful entry for permanent residence of the declarant above named on the date stated for the declaration of intention, has been received by me, and that the photograph affixed to the duplicate and triplicate hereof is a likeness of the declarant.

[SEAL]

R. S. Zimmerman, Clerk U. S. District Court,
Clerk of the Southern District of California
By
FORM N-315
U. S. DEPARTMENT OF JUSTICE 610—16156 U. S. GOVERNMENT PRINTING OFFICE
IMMIGRATION AND NATURALIZATION SERVICE
(Edition of 5-13-41)

Reynalda Martinez

Declaration of Intention-Reynalda Martinez

NATURALIZATION RECORDS

On page 30, we have reproduced Reynalda's *Petition for Naturalization*, which was filed several years later. The detailed testimony required of immigrants in such documents would be most useful to a grandchild or great-grandchild who may never have known or met their immigrant ancestor.

Every line of a naturalization document may provide clues for your research and it is important for you to carefully analyze each item for such information. In Reynalda's petition for naturalization, you should note that she claims to have resided in the state of California since 1919. The significance of this revelation is that you may want to search the 1920 federal census for this individual.

The next document, reproduced on Page 31, shows Reynalda's *Certificate of Arrival*. After 1906, each applicant for naturalization was required to show lawful admission for permanent residence in the United States. A government official would go back to the original border crossing manifests to verify that the immigrant had actually arrived at the place and date indicated in their original declaration document. At that point, the official would issue a *Certificate of Registry*.

According to this document, Reynalda Nevarez, aka Reynalda Martinez, had traveled by buggy across the Mexican border on April 15, 1912 at El Paso, Texas. This document attests to the existence of the actual border-crossing records at the El Paso Immigration and Naturalization Office, showing that Reynalda did indeed cross the border almost three decades earlier.

The final step in the naturalization process would then be a court order, acknowledging that Reynalda had complied with the requirements for citizenship and was thus awarded naturalization. Reynalda was then issued a *Naturalization Certificate,* which verified her citizenship. This document, which has been reproduced on page 32, represents the final stage in the citizenship process. Thus a process that began in September 1941 came to an end on November 8, 1946 with Reynalda's certification as a citizen.

114

ORIGINAL
(To be retained by
Clerk of Court)

UNITED STATES OF AMERICA

No. 129784

PETITION FOR NATURALIZATION
[Under General Provisions of the Nationality Act of 1940 (Public, No. 853, 76th Cong.)]

To the Honorable the DISTRICT Court of THE UNITED STATES at LOS ANGELES, CALIF.

This petition for naturalization, hereby made and filed, respectfully shows:

(1) My full, true, and correct name is REYNALDA MARTINEZ (nee Mesa-Navarar).

(2) My present place of residence is 515 S. Chicago St. Los Angeles 33. occupation Housewife

(3) I am 53 years old. (5) I was born on August 27, 1892 in Tepehuanes, Durango, Mexico

(4) My personal description is as follows: Sex female, color White, complexion dark, color of eyes brn, color of hair black, height 5 1, weight 124 pounds, visible distinctive marks none, race white,

present nationality Mexico. (7) I am married; the name of my husband is Jose Martinez

we were married on October 7, 1922 at Santa Ana, California

he or she was born at Chihuahua, Mexico on unknown

and entered the United States at El Paso, Texas on 1906

and now resides with me.

(8) I have one children, and the name, sex, date and place of birth, and present place of residence of each of said children who is living, are as follows:

Jose X born Jan. 6, 1912 in Tepehuanes, Mexico. res. Los Angeles, Calif.

(9) My last place of foreign residence was Ciudad Juarez, Mexico. (10) I emigrated to the United States from
Ciudad Juarez, Mexico (11) My lawful entry for permanent residence in the United States was
at El Paso, Texas under the name of Reynalda Navares now Reynalda Martinez
on April 15, 19 on the Buggy

(12) Since my lawful entry for permanent residence I have not been absent from the United States, for a period or periods of 6 months or longer, as follows:

DEPARTED FROM THE UNITED STATES			RETURNED TO THE UNITED STATES		
Port	Date (Month, day, year)	Vessel or Other Means of Conveyance	Port	Date (Month, day, year)	Vessel or Other Means of Conveyance

(13) I declared my intention to become a citizen of the United States on September 29, 1941 in the District
Court at United States at Los Angeles, California

(14) It is my intention in good faith to become a citizen of the United States and to renounce absolutely and forever all allegiance and fidelity to any foreign prince, potentate, state, or sovereignty of whom or which at this time I am a subject or citizen, and it is my intention to reside permanently in the United States. (15) I am not, and have not been for the period of at least 10 years immediately preceding the date of this petition, an anarchist; nor a believer in the unlawful destruction of property, or sabotage; nor a disbeliever in or opposed to organized government; nor a member of or affiliated with any organization or body of persons teaching disbelief in or opposition to organized government; (16) I am able to speak the English language (unless physically unable to do so). (17) I am not, and have not been during all of the periods required by law, attached to the principles of the Constitution of the United States and well disposed to the good order and happiness of the United States.

citizen of the United States for the term of 5 years at least immediately preceding the date of this petition, to wit, since April 15, 1912

and continuously in the State in which this petition is made for the term of 6 months at least immediately preceding the date of this petition, to wit, since
1919 (18) I have not heretofore made petition for naturalization: No. _____

_____ at _____ in the _____

Court, and such petition was dismissed or denied by that Court for the following reasons and causes, to wit:

and the cause of such dismissal or denial has since been cured or removed.

(20) Attached hereto and made a part of this, my petition for naturalization, are my declaration of intention to become a citizen of the United States (if such declaration of intention is required by the naturalization law), a certificate of arrival from the Immigration and Naturalization Service of my said lawful entry into the United States for permanent residence (if the naturalization law requires such certificate of arrival), and the affidavits of at least two verifying witnesses required by law.

(21) Wherefore, I, your petitioner for naturalization, pray that I may be admitted a citizen of the United States of America, and that my name be changed to _____

Edna Martinez

(22) I, aforesaid petitioner, do swear (affirm) that I know the contents of this petition for naturalization subscribed by me, that the same are true to the best of my own knowledge, except as to matters therein stated to be alleged upon information and belief, and that as to those matters I believe them to be true, and that this petition is signed by me with my full, true name. SO HELP ME GOD.

X *Reynalda Martinez*

Petition for Naturalization-Reynalda Martinez

U. S. DEPARTMENT OF JUSTICE
IMMIGRATION AND NATURALIZATION SERVICE

No. 23 R 103990

CERTIFICATE OF ARRIVAL

I HEREBY CERTIFY that the immigration records show that the alien named below arrived at the port, on the date, and in the manner shown, and was lawfully admitted to the United States of America for permanent residence.

Name: Reynalda Nevares now Reynalda Martinez
Port of entry: El Paso, Texas
Date: April 15, 1912   VFP   1282355
Manner of arrival: Buggy

I FURTHER CERTIFY that this certificate of arrival is issued under authority of, and in conformity with, the provisions of the Nationality Act of 1940 (Pub., No. 853, 76th Cong.), solely for the use of the alien herein named and only for naturalization purposes.

IN WITNESS WHEREOF, this certificate of arrival is issued _____ SEP 11 1941

CERTIFICATE OF REGISTRY ISSUED

LEMUEL B. SCHOFIELD,
Special Assistant to the Attorney General.

By *E.E. Salisbury*

Chief, Certifications Branch.

Form N-228

U. S. GOVERNMENT PRINTING OFFICE 16—19161

se

Certificate of Arrival for Reynalda Martinez

31

ORIGINAL
TO BE GIVEN TO
THE PERSON NATURALIZED

No. 6640590

Petition No. 129764

Personal description of holder as of date of naturalization: Age 54 years; sex Female
complexion Dark color of eyes Brown color of hair Black height 5 feet 1 inches
weight 124 pounds; visible distinctive marks None
Marital status Married former nationality Mexican
I certify that the description above given is true, and that the photograph affixed hereto is a likeness of me.

Edna Martinez
(Complete and true signature of holder)

UNITED STATES OF AMERICA
SOUTHERN DIST. OF CALIFORNIA } ss:

Be it known, that at a term of the District Court of The United States held pursuant to law at Los Angeles
on NOV - 8 1946 the Court having found that ** EDNA MARTINEZ **
then residing at 513 S. Chicago St., Los Angeles, Calif.
intends to reside permanently in the United States (when so required by the Naturalization Laws of the United States), had in all other respects complied with the applicable provisions of such naturalization laws, and was entitled to be admitted to citizenship, thereupon ordered that such person be and (s)he was admitted as a citizen of the United States of America.
In testimony whereof the seal of the court is hereunto affixed this 8th
day of November in the year of our Lord nineteen hundred and forty-six and of our Independence the one hundred and seventy-first

Edmund L. Smith
Clerk of the U. S. District Court
By [signature] Deputy Clerk.

Seal

It is a violation of the U.S. Code (and punishable as such) to copy, print, photograph, or otherwise illegally use this certificate.

Naturalization Certificate-Edna Martinez

NATURALIZATION RECORDS

On page 34, we move on to a new set of naturalization documents. We have reproduced the November 7, 1936 *Declaration of Intention* for one Pablo Dominguez of Rush County, Kansas. Mr. Dominguez, a native of Zacatecas, Mexico, declared his intent to become a citizen in Lacrosse, Rush County, Kansas. Although the word Zacatecas was misspelled, this document provides us with a great deal of information on this individual and his family.

On page 35, we can see Pablo Dominguez's *Petition for Naturalization*, signed three years later on September 25, 1939, in which two witnesses came forth to speak of Pablo's moral character and recommend him for citizenship. The third document for Pablo Dominguez, reproduced on page 36, is Pablo's *Certificate of Arrival*, in which D. W. MacCormack, an INS official, certified that the immigration records at El Paso showed that Pablo had indeed passed through that port of entry on October 25, 1926 by railway.

If your ancestor jumped ship or crossed the Mexican border without being tallied or recorded by border officials, it is likely that a *Certificate of Registration* was never issued. Not having been legally admitted to the United States, this class of aliens was not in a position to acquire American citizenship.

However, in 1929, Congress recognized the position in which these people found themselves and decided to provide a remedy. In an act that became effective on July 1, 1929, Congress declared "that a record of registry may be made for any alien in whose case no immigration record of arrival exists, who entered the United States prior to June 3, 1921, has resided in the United States continuously since such entry, is a person of good moral character, and is not subject to deportation."[2]

This act gave Victor Villagrana the opportunity to become a citizen. On page 37, we have reproduced the *Petition for Naturalization* of Victor Villagrana, a native of Zacatecas who crossed the border at El Paso on

---

[2] United States Labor Department, *Eighteenth Annual Report of the Secretary of Labor for the Fiscal Year Ended June 30, 1930* (Washington, D.C.: United States Government Printing Office, 1930), p. 77.

TRIPLICATE
(To be given to declarant)

No. ....423...

UNITED STATES OF AMERICA

DECLARATION OF INTENTION
(Invalid for all purposes seven years after the date hereof)

State of Kansas

In the ....District....... Court

Rush County

ss.

of Rush County at LaCrosse, Kansas

I, Pablo Dominguez

now residing at .... LaCrosse .... Rush, ... Kansas

occupation Section Laborer , aged 49 years, do declare on oath that my personal description is :

Sex Male , color Dark , complexion Dark , color of eyes Brown ,

color of hair Black , height 5 feet 5 inches; weight pounds, visible distinctive marks

small scar on chin

race Mexican , nationality Mexican

I was born in Tucubeoya , Mexico , on Dec. 27, 1882

I am married. The name of my wife or husband is Dionicio

we were married on Oct. 15, 1920, at Ciudad Juarez, Mexico , she or he was

born at Barral , Mexico on Oct. 9, 1895 , entered the United States

at El Pasco , Texas Oct. 25, 1922 for permanent residence therein, and now

resides at LaCrosse, Kansas I have 3 children, and the name, date and place of birth,

and place of residence of each of said children are as follows: Isaac, born Jan. 29, 1915, Barral, Mexico, resides at LaCrosse, Mexico, " Oct. 20, 1917 " , Socorro " May 20, 1923 Chihuahua,

I have not heretofore made a declaration of intention: Number .... on ....

at ....

my last foreign residence was Chihuahua, Mexico

I emigrated to the United States of America from Juarez Mexico

my lawful entry for permanent residence in the United States was at El Paso, Texas

under the name of Pablo Dominguez , on Oct. 25, 1922

on the vessel U.S. Ry Co

I will, before being admitted to citizenship, renounce forever all allegiance and fidelity to any foreign prince, potentate, state, or sovereignty, and particularly, by name, to the prince, potentate, state, or sovereignty of which I may be at the time of admission a citizen or subject; I am not an anarchist; I am not a polygamist nor a believer in the practice of polygamy; and it is my intention in good faith to become a citizen of the United States of America and to reside permanently therein; and I certify that the photograph affixed to the duplicate and triplicate hereof is a likeness of me: So help me God.

Pablo Dominguez

Subscribed and sworn to before me in the office of the Clerk of said Court,

at LaCrosse, Kansas this 7th day of Nov.,

anno Domini 19 6 . Certification No. 6-9797 from the Commissioner of Immigration and Naturalization showing the lawful entry of the declarant for permanent residence on the date stated above, has been received by me. The photograph affixed to the duplicate and triplicate hereof is a likeness of the declarant.

[SEAL]

Clerk of the District Court.

By .... , Deputy Clerk.

Form 2202-L-A
U. S. DEPARTMENT OF LABOR
IMMIGRATION AND NATURALIZATION SERVICE

No. 30066

Declaration of Intention-Pablo Dominguez

ORIGINAL
(To be retained by clerk)

UNITED STATES OF AMERICA

No. 361

PETITION FOR NATURALIZATION

To the Honorable the __District__ Court of __Rush County,__ at __LaCrosse Kansas__

The petition of __Pablo Dominguez__ hereby filed, respectfully shows:

(1) My place of residence is __LaCrosse, Kansas__ (2) My occupation is __Section Laborer__

(3) I was born in __Zacatecas, Zac. Mexico, December 27, 1862__ race is __White__

(4) I declared my intention to become a citizen of the United States on __Nov 7, 1936__ in the __District__ Court of __Rush County,__ at __LaCrosse, Kansas__

(5) I am __married__. The name of my wife or husband is __Dionicia__ we were married on __Oct 15, 1926__ at __Zacatecas, Mexico__ she was born at __Parral,Chi,Mexico__ on __Oct 9, 1893__ entered the United States at __El Paso, Texas,__ on __Oct 25, 1926__ for permanent residence therein, and now resides at __with me__ I have __Kno__ children, and the same date, and place of birth, and place of residence of each of said children are as follows

(6) My last foreign residence was __Zacatecas, Mexico__ I emigrated to the United States of America from __Zacatecas, Mexico__ My lawful entry for permanent residence in the United States was at __El Paso, Texas__ under the name of __Pablo Dominguez__ on __Oct. 25, 1926__ on the vessel __E.P.E. Ry Co.__

(7) I am not a disbeliever in or opposed to organized government or a member of or affiliated with any organization or body of persons teaching disbelief in or opposed to organized government. I am not a polygamist nor a believer in the practice of polygamy. I am attached to the principles of the Constitution of the United States and well disposed to the good order and happiness of the United States. It is my intention to become a citizen of the United States and to renounce absolutely and forever all allegiance and fidelity to any foreign prince, potentate, state, or sovereignty, and particularly to

of whom I am at this time a subject (or citizen), and it is my intention to reside permanently in the United States (8) I am able to speak the English language (9) I have resided continuously in the United States of America for the term of 5 years at least immediately preceding the date of this petition, to wit, since __October 25, 1926__ and in the County of __Rush__ this State, continuously next preceding the date of this petition, since __October 25, 1926__ being a residence within said county of at least 6 months next preceding the date of this petition. (10) I have __no__ heretofore made petition for naturalization: No. _____ at _____ and such petition was denied by that Court for the following reasons and causes, to wit:

and the cause of such denial has since been cured or removed.

Attached hereto and made a part of this, my petition for citizenship, are my declaration of intention to become a citizen of the United States, certificate from the Department of Labor of my said arrival, and the affidavits of the two verifying witnesses required by law. Wherefore, I, your petitioner, pray that I may be admitted a citizen of the United States of America, and that my name be changed to

I, __Pablo Dominguez__ do swear (affirm) that I know the contents of this petition for naturalization subscribed by me, that the same are true to the best of my own knowledge, except as to matters therein stated to be alleged upon information and belief, and that as to those matters I believe them to be true, and that this petition was signed by me with my full, true name: SO HELP ME GOD.

Pablo Dominguez

AFFIDAVITS OF WITNESSES

__Albert J. Smith,__ residing at __LaCrosse, Kansas__ occupation __Merchant__ and __William A. Hayes__ residing at __LaCrosse, Kansas__ occupation __Banker.__ each being severally, duly, and respectively sworn, deposes and says: I am a citizen of the United States of America, I have personally known and have been acquainted in the United States with __PABLO DOMINGUEZ__ the petitioner above mentioned, since __Jan 1, 1927__ and that to my personal knowledge the petitioner has resided in the United States continuously preceding the date of filing this petition, of which this affidavit is a part, to wit, since the date last mentioned and at __LaCrosse__ in the County of __Rush__ in this State, in which the above-entitled petition is made, continuously since __Jan 1, 1927__ and that I have personal knowledge that the petitioner is and during all such periods has been a person of good moral character, attached to the principles of the Constitution of the United States, and well disposed to the good order and happiness of the United States, and in my opinion the petitioner is in every way qualified to be admitted a citizen of the United States. I do swear (affirm) that the statements of fact I have made in this affidavit of this petition have been supported by me are true, to the best of my knowledge and belief.

Albert Smith   *William A Hayes*

Subscribed and sworn to before me by the above-named petitioner and witnesses in the respective forms of each shown above in the office of Clerk of said Court at __LaCrosse Kansas__ this __28__ day of __Sept__ Anno Domini 19__39__. I hereby certify that Certificate of Arrival No. __A-5797__ from the Department of Labor, showing the lawful entry for permanent residence of the petitioner above named, together with Declaration of Intention No. __422__ of such petitioner, has been by me filed with, attached to, and made a part of this petition, on this date.

By _____ Clerk _____ Deputy Clerk

No. 208817

U.S. DEPARTMENT OF LABOR
IMMIGRATION AND NATURALIZATION SERVICE
Form 2204—L

Petition for Naturalization-Pablo Dominguez

U. S. DEPARTMENT OF LABOR
IMMIGRATION AND NATURALIZATION SERVICE

No. 16....5707...................

CERTIFICATE OF ARRIVAL

I HEREBY CERTIFY that the immigration records show that the alien named below arrived at the por on the date, and in the manner shown, and was lawfully admitted to the United States of America fo permanent residence.

Name: Pablo Dominguez
Port of entry: El Paso, Texas
Date: Oct. 25, 1926
Manner of arrival: E.P.E. Ry. Co.

RECEIVE
OCT   9
Immigration and Na
Service

I FURTHER CERTIFY that this certificate of arrival is issued under authority of, and in conformity wit the provisions of the Act of June 29, 1906, as amended, solely for the use of the alien herein named and on for naturalization purposes.

IN WITNESS WHEREOF, this Certificate of Arrival is issued

OCT 5 - 1936

hls

D. W. MacCORMACK,
Commissioner.

Form 561   U. S. GOVERNMENT PRINTING OFFICE   14—2001

Certificate of Arrival-Pablo Dominguez

UNITED STATES DEPARTMENT OF JUSTICE
IMMIGRATION AND NATURALIZATION SERVICE

Form approved
Budget Bureau No. 43-R062.3

ORIGINAL
(To be retained
by Clerk of Court)

UNITED STATES OF AMERICA

PETITION FOR NATURALIZATION

No. ....

Filed under ....316............

To the Honorable the ....U. S. DISTRICT COURT FOR THE SOUTHERN (NORTHERN)........ at ....

This petition for naturalization, hereby made and filed, respectfully shows:

(1) My full, true, and correct name is ....VICTOR VILLAGRANA........

(2) My present place of residence is ....2710 E. Victor St. Los Angeles 11........ (3) My occupation ....
........Unemployed........ (4) I was born on .... in .... Mexico 2nd........

(5) My personal description is as follows: Sex .... complexion .... color of eyes .... color of hair ....
color of hair .... height 5 feet 6 inches, weight 140 pounds, visible distinctive marks Slight bump on bridge of nose
race .... subject or national Mexico (8) I am .... SINGLE ....

(7a) ....

(7b) ....

(8) I have NO children, and the name, sex, date and place of birth, and present place of residence of each of said children who is living, are as follows:

....

(9) My lawful admission for permanent residence in the United States was at El Paso, Texas ....
under the name of ....Victor Benitez Villagrana........ on 6/1970 ....
on the On Foot ....

(10) Since my lawful admission for permanent residence I have not been absent from the United States, for a period or periods of 6 months or longer, except as follows:

DEPARTED FROM THE UNITED STATES			RETURNED TO THE UNITED STATES		
PORT	DATE (Month, day, year)	VESSEL OR OTHER MEANS OF CONVEYANCE	PORT	DATE (Month, day, year)	VESSEL OR OTHER MEANS OF CONVEYANCE

(11) It is my intention in good faith to become a citizen of the United States and to renounce absolutely and entirely all allegiance and fidelity to any foreign prince, potentate, state, or sovereignty of whom or which at that time I am a subject or citizen. (12) It is my intention to reside permanently in the United States. (13) ....

(14) I have resided continuously in the United States since 6/15/04 .... and continuously in the State in which this petition is made for the term of 6 months at least immediately preceding the date of this petition and I have been physically present in the United States for at least one-half of the 5 year period immediately preceding the date of this petition. (17) I have not heretofore made petition for naturalization No. ....

(18) Attached hereto and made a part of this, my petition for naturalization, are the affidavits of at least two verifying witnesses required by law.

(19) Wherefore, I, your petitioner for naturalization, pray that I may be admitted a citizen of the United States of America, and that my name be changed to None .... I, aforesaid petitioner, do swear (affirm) that I know the contents of this petition for naturalization subscribed by me, and that the same are true to the best of my knowledge and belief and that this petition is signed by me with my full, true name. SO HELP ME GOD.

ALIEN REGISTRATION NO. A 2 069 276 .... *Victor Villagrana*

Form N-405
(Rev. 12-1-66)

Petition for Naturalization-Victor Villagrana

June 15, 1904. When Victor crossed the border in 1904, border-crossings along the Mexican border were not recorded at all. Until 1929, this gentleman would not have qualified for American citizenship although he had resided in the country for more than two decades.[3]

It is also important to note that Victor's *Alien Registration Number* is indicated at the bottom of the document. The significance and value of this number will be discussed in the next chapter.

The final document in this section, reproduced on page 39, is a *Petition for Naturalization* for Nicolasa Elizalde, aka Nicolasa Juarez nee Garcia. Nicolasa had also crossed the border at El Paso during a time when Mexican nationals were not tallied by border officials.[4]

Nicolasa's petition, filed during the 1940s, states that Nicolasa was born in Durango, Mexico. As a matter of fact, Nicolasa was actually born in Zacatecas, but had lived in Durango for a few months before crossing the border as an infant in the care of her parents. The significance of Nicolasa's document is that we should always be aware of the fact that some information may be incorrect.

There are several exceptions to the old naturalization policy that you should be aware of. One is called *derivative citizenship*, which was granted to the wives and minor children of naturalized men from 1790 to 1922. Hence, a husband's naturalization in 1920 would have automatically made citizens of his wife and minor children. Up until that time, an alien woman who married an American citizen would also become a citizen automatically. Up until 1940, children under the age of 21 automatically became naturalized citizens upon the naturalization of their father.

---

[3] The naturalization document for Victor Villagrana have been made available through the courtesy of Rebecca Alviso and Margaret Nevarez.
[4] The naturalization document for Nicolasa Elizalde have been made available through the courtesy of Rebecca Alviso and Margaret Nevarez.

ORIGINAL
(To be retained by
Clerk of Court)

UNITED STATES OF AMERICA

No.

PETITION FOR NATURALIZATION

[Of a Married Person, under Sec. 310(a) (b) of the Nationality Act of 1940 (54 Stat. 1144-1145)]

To the Honorable the DISTRICT Court of THE UNITED STATES at LOS ANGELES, CALIF.

This petition for naturalization, hereby made and filed pursuant to Section 310a (a) (b), of the Nationality Act of 1940, respectfully shows:

(1) My full, true, and correct name is NICOLASA ELIZALDE (Nicolasa Juarez) nee Garcia

(2) My present place of residence is 1027 Alpine St, Los Angeles, 12, Cal. My occupation is Housewife

(4) I am 40 years old. (5) I was born on Sept. 10, 1904 in Durango, Mexico

(6) My personal description is as follows: Sex fem, color white, complexion med, color of eyes brn, color of hair brn, height 5 feet 1 inches, weight 155 pounds, visible distinctive marks 2 moles on lft cheek, white, race Mexico, present nationality Mexico

(7) I am married; the name of my wife or husband is Antonio Elizalde we were married on May 1, 1937 at Los Angeles, Calif. who or she was born at Morenci, Arizona on Jan. 16, 1893,

entered the United States at on for permanent residence in the United States, and now resides at

with me and was naturalized on at certificate No., or became a citizen by

(8) I have 4 children, and the name, sex, date and place of birth, and present place of residence of each of said children who is living, are as follows:

Trinidad(f)May 22, 1921-San Pedro,Calif;Teresa(f)Oct. 15, 1922,Los Angeles, Calif;
Porfirio(m)March 6, 1928-Los Angeles, Calif;Ofelia(f)11-28-1941-L.A. Calif;
All reside with me

(9) My last place of foreign residence was Durango, Mexico (10) I emigrated to the United States from Durango, Mexico

(11) My lawful entry for permanent residence in the United States was at El Paso, Texas under the name

of Nicolasa Garcia on May 15, 1905 on the on foot

(12) Since my lawful entry for permanent residence I have not been absent from the United States, for a period or periods of 6 months or longer, as follows:

DEPARTED FROM THE UNITED STATES			RETURNED TO THE UNITED STATES		
PORT	DATE (Month, day, year)	VESSEL OR OTHER MEANS OF CONVEYANCE	PORT	DATE (Month, day, year)	VESSEL OR OTHER MEANS OF CONVEYANCE

(15) I have resided continuously in the United States for the term of 3 years at least immediately preceding the date of this petition, to wit, since May 15, 1905 (19) I have not heretofore made petition for naturalization

number on at in the (Name of court)

Court, and such petition was dismissed or denied by that Court for the following reasons and causes, to wit:

(21) Wherefore, I, your petitioner for naturalization, pray that I may be admitted a citizen of the United States of America, and that my name be changed to no change

Nicolasa Elizalde

Petition for Naturalization-Nicolasa Elizalde

39

NATURALIZATION RECORDS

You can request naturalization papers issued after 1906 from the National Archives, also known as NARA (National Archives Regional Administration). If you are interested in exploring the various NARA websites to find out about the various facility locations, holdings, or policies, you might start with the following National Archives website: *http://www.archives.gov/facilities/index.html.*

NARA's Pacific Region, which is located in Laguna Niguel, California, is responsible for the immigration records of the southern California area, as well as Arizona and a part of Nevada. Their address is:

NARA (Pacific Region)
24000 Avila Road, 1st Floor
P.O. Box 6719
Laguna Niguel, California 92677-3497

NARA's Southwest Region, centered at Fort Worth, covering Arkansas, Louisiana, Oklahoma, and Texas, is at the following address:

NARA (Southwest Region)
P.O. Box 6216
Fort Worth, Texas 76115-0216

You are able to Email requests for naturalization records to many of the NARA facilities. However, if you decide to Email your request to NARA, please make sure that you give as much information as possible. Approximate dates and locations are better than giving no information at all. In addition, give your address and daytime phone number.

The naturalization documents reproduced in this chapter give us a very clear idea of what we may learn by exploring this avenue of research. However, many Mexican immigrants never chose the path of citizenship and, as a result, no naturalization records exist for those individuals. Although this represents a significant disadvantage to the Mexican-American family historian, there are other government documents that may help you to fill in the gaps. These alternatives will be discussed in the following chapters.

Chapter 5
Alien Registration Records
Donna Morales

If your ancestors never became citizens, you will, of course, be unable to locate naturalization records for them. As a result, you may become frustrated in your attempts to locate relevant documents relating to your family. But naturalization papers are not the only means by which you can locate a place of origin for your family in Mexico. If your immigrant ancestor was living in the United States during the 1940s, you can write to the INS office in Washington to request his or her Alien Registration Form.

The United States launched the *Alien Registration Program* in July, 1940. The *Alien Registration Act of 1940*, enacted by the Seventy-Sixth Congress, was approved by President Roosevelt on June 28, 1940. The provisions of this act required that every alien resident of the United States over the age of fourteen who was in the country for at least thirty days must register at his or her local Post Office between August 27, 1940 and December 26, 1940. To fulfill this responsibility, the aliens were fingerprinted and filled out a two-page form (the AR-2).   They were also required to answer under oath inquiries concerning the date and place of their entry into the United States and any activities in which they were engaged.[1]

The registration records were serially numbered and forwarded by the post office employees to the INS for statistical coding, indexing, and filing.   Once the AR-2 had been processed, an AR-3, or *Alien Registration Receipt Card*, was torn off and mailed to the registered alien. From that point on, the alien was required by law to carry that card on his person at all times.

---

[1] United States Labor Department, *Twenty-Eighth Annual Report of the Secretary of Labor for the Fiscal Year Ended June 30, 1940* (Washington, D.C.: United States Government Printing Office, 1940), pp. 119-120.

ALIEN REGISTRATION RECORDS

Many of the people who registered in 1940 were long-time residents of the United States who had simply not become citizens, for whatever reasons. Several members of my family who were born in Mexico and came to the United States between 1909 and 1912 fell into this classification.

On page 43, you will see the Alien Registration Form for Juana Luevano de Morales, my paternal grandmother, who never applied for American citizenship. This form provides us with a great deal of information about my grandmother, including her address, her nationality, her height and physical description, and her occupation.

For some reason, my grandmother, who was then in her sixties, did not give her full date of birth. Instead, Juana simply stated that she had been born in Villa Hidalgo in the Mexican state of Jalisco in 1888. In her registration, she claimed that she had first crossed the border into the United States on February 20, 1906. How many times Juana actually crossed the frontier is unknown, but she stated that she crossed the border for the last time at Eagle Pass, Texas on March 15, 1912.

Unfortunately, an older person who had been in the United States for decades may have not remembered their exact date of entry. This appears to have been the case for Juana. At a later date, we located Juana's border-crossing manifest, which states that she actually crossed the Mexican border at Eagle Pass on November 19, 1912, eight months after her stated date of March 15. The location and utilization of border-crossing records for genealogical research will be discussed in greater detail in our next chapter.

Sometimes uneducated, illiterate immigrants did not know their correct year of birth. On page 44, we have reproduced Juana Luevano's 1885 baptism record from Villa Hidalgo.

Form AR-2
OFFICE USE

6872610

COPY

UNITED STATES DEPARTMENT OF JUSTICE
IMMIGRATION AND NATURALIZATION SERVICE

ALIEN REGISTRATION FORM

OFFICE USE

1. ☆(a) My name is _____ Juana _____ (none) _____ Luevano vda. de Morales
(FIRST NAME) (MIDDLE NAME) (LAST NAME)

☆(b) I entered the United States under the name of _____ Juana L. Morales

☆(c) I have also been known by the following names
(include maiden name if a married woman,
professional names, nicknames, and aliases): _____ Juana Luevano (maiden name)

2. ☆(a) I live at _____ 1028 S. 22nd St., _____ Kansas City, _____ Wyandotte, _____ Kansas
(STREET ADDRESS OR RURAL ROUTE) (CITY) (COUNTY) (STATE)

☆(b) My post-office address is _____ Same as above
(POST OFFICE) (STATE)

3. ☆(a) I was born on _____ Unknown _____ Unknown _____ 1888
(MONTH) (DAY) (YEAR)

☆(b) I was born in (or near) _____ Villa Hidalgo, _____ Jalisco, _____ Mexico
(CITY) (PROVINCE) (COUNTRY)

4. ☆ I am a citizen or subject of _____ Mexico
(COUNTRY)

5. ☆(a) I am (check one): _____ ☆(b) My marital status is (check one):
Male ☐¹ Female ☒² _____ Single ☐¹ Married ☐² Widowed ☒³ Divorced ☐⁴
☆(c) My race is (check one): White ☒¹ Negro ☐² Japanese ☐³ Chinese ☐⁴ Other

6. I am _5_ feet, _0_ inches in height, weigh _112_ pounds, have _Grey_ hair and _Brown_ eyes.
(COLOR) (COLOR)

7. ☆(a) I last arrived in the United States at _____ Eagle Pass, Texas _____ on _____ March 15, 1912
(PORT OR PLACE OF ENTRY) (MONTH, DAY AND YEAR)

☆(b) I came in by _____ on foot across the bridge.
(NAME OF VESSEL, STEAMSHIP COMPANY, OR OTHER MEANS OF TRANSPORTATION)

☆(c) I came as a (check one): Passenger ☐¹ Crew member ☐² Stowaway ☐³ Other _Pedestrian_
☆(d) I entered the United States as a (check one): Permanent resident ☒¹ Visitor ☐² Student ☐³
Treaty merchant ☐⁴ Seaman ☐⁵ Official of a foreign government ☐⁶ Employee of a
foreign government official ☐⁷ Other

☆(e) I first arrived in the United States on _____ February, _____ 20, _____ 1906
(MONTH) (DAY) (YEAR)

8. ☆(a) I have lived in the United States a total of _42_ years

☆(b) I expect to remain in the United States _permanently._
(PERMANENTLY, OR DURATION OF EXPECTED STAY)

9. (a) My usual occupation is _Housewife_ (b) My present occupation is _Housewife_

☆(c) My employer (or registering parent or guardian) is _____ None
(NAME)

whose address is _____
(STREET ADDRESS OR RURAL ROUTE) (CITY) (STATE)

and whose business is _____

All items must be answered by persons 14 years of age, or older. For children under 14 years of age, only the items marked with
a star (☆) must be answered by the parent or guardian. All answers must be accurate and complete.

Alien Registration Form of Juana Luevano de Morales

Juana Luevano Baptism, 1885-Villa Hidalgo, Jalisco

ALIEN REGISTRATION RECORDS

The *Registros Parroquiales* (Parish Registers) at the small town of Villa Hidalgo, a few miles south of the border between the states of Jalisco and Aguascalientes, were filmed by the Genealogical Society of Utah in 1977. The records for *La Santisima Trinidad Church* in Villa Hidalgo from 1814 to 1955 are available on 33 rolls of microfilm through the Family History Library. [2]

According to this church record, Juana Luevano was baptized on September 29, 1885, which tells us that her year of birth on the alien registration form was off by three years. The translation of this document reads as follows:

> *In the Parish of Paso de Sotos on the 29th of September of 1885, I, Father Estevan Agredano... baptized solemnly and poured Holy Oil and Sacred Chrism on JUANA, who was born on the 27th day at seven in the morning in this place, the legitimate daughter of Tiburcio Luevano and Manuela Martinez. Paternal grandparents: Pablo Luevano and Manuela Serna. Maternal grandparents: Timoteo Martinez and Fermina Rubalcaba. Godparents: Paulin Diaz and Epifania Aguallo, whom I advised of their spiritual and parental obligation,. In witness thereof, I signed it.*

It is important to note that this baptism, in addition to listing Juana's parents, also lists her *abuelos paternos* (paternal grandparents) and *abuelos maternos* (maternal grandparents). This format was common throughout many parts of Mexico, starting about 1800, and gives an enormous advantage to people who are tracing Mexican lineages. Unfortunately, some states of Mexico – such as Guanajuato and Michoacán – did not generally follow this style.

---

[2] Reprinted by permission. Copyright © 2000 by the Intellectual Reserve, Inc. The 1885 baptism records for the church in Villa Hidalgo, Jalisco are located on Family History Library Microfilm #1155557.

ALIEN REGISTRATION RECORDS

On page 47, we have reproduced the Alien Registration Form for my maternal uncle, Pablo Dominguez. When Uncle Pablo registered at his local Post Office in 1940, he stated that he was born on April 2, 1905 in the small town of Santa Monica in the Mexican state of Zacatecas. This town is so small that you won't be able to find it on most maps, but it belongs to the municipio of Sain Alto in northwestern Zacatecas. Uncle Pablo stated that he had arrived in the United States on November 19, 1909 by electric railway at the El Paso port of entry. Through this document, we learn that Pablo worked as a painter for the Santa Fe Railway.

It is interesting to note that he crossed the border under the name Pablo Salaz. As a matter of fact, several members of my mother's family apparently entered the country using this surname. However, the family name in Mexico was Dominguez, not Salaz. The use of the second surname may have been related to legal problems in the Old Country.

On page 48, we have reproduced the baptism record for Pablo Dominguez. This document, which we located through the Family History Library Catalog, was obtained from the Parish Registers of Rio de Medina, Zacatecas, contained on Film Number 439817. The translation of this document reads as follows:[3]

> *In the Chapel of the Hacienda de Rio de Medina of the Parish of Fresnillo on the 8th day of April in 1905, I, Father Lucio Huerta, with permission from Father Manuel Avila González, baptized solemnly and poured Holy Oil and Sacred Chrism on a boy born in Paso de la Cruz on the 2nd day of the same [month] at 8 in the morning, whom I gave the name Pablo, legitimate son of Geronimo Dominguez and Luisa Lujan. Paternal grandparents: Aniceto Dominguez and Martina Segovia. Maternal grandparents: Geronimo Lujan and Lucia Fraile. Godparents: Nicolas Medrano and Rosario Natera, whom I advised of their parental and spiritual duties. In witness thereof, they signed it.*

Form AR-2
OFFICE USE

5126098

UNITED STATES DEPARTMENT OF JUSTICE
IMMIGRATION AND NATURALIZATION SERVICE

ALIEN REGISTRATION FORM

	OFFICE USE

1. ☆(a) My name is .... Pablo .... (none) .... Dominguez
    (FIRST NAME) (MIDDLE NAME) (LAST NAME)

   ☆(b) I entered the United States under the name of Pablo Salaz

   ☆(c) I have also been known by the following names ...... Paul Dominguez
   (include maiden name if a married woman,
   professional names, nicknames, and aliases):

2. ☆(a) I live at .... Turner .... Wyandotte .... Kansas
    (STREET ADDRESS OR RURAL ROUTE) (CITY) (COUNTY) (STATE)

   ☆(b) My post-office address is .. P. O. Box 166 .... Turner .... Kansas
   (POST OFFICE) (STATE)

3. ☆(a) I was born on .... April 2 1905
   (MONTH) (DAY) (YEAR)

   ☆(b) I was born in (or near) .. Santa Monica .... Zac. .... Mexico
   (CITY) (PROVINCE) (COUNTRY)

4. ☆ I am a citizen or subject of nonci last of Mexico
   (COUNTRY)

5. ☆(a) I am a (check one): Male..X..[1] Female..[2]   ☆(b) My marital status is (check one): Single..[1] Married..[2] Widowed..[3] Divorced..[4]

   ☆(c) My race is (check one): White..X..[1] Negro..[2] Japanese..[3] Chinese..[4] Other Mexican

6. I am 5 feet, 3 inches in height, weigh 149 pounds, have black hair and brown eyes.
   (COLOR) (COLOR)

7. ☆(a) I last arrived in the United States at El Paso, Tex. on Nov. 19, 1909
   (PORT OR PLACE OF ENTRY) (MONTH, DAY AND YEAR)

   ☆(b) I came in by El Paso, Electric Railway
   (NAME OF VESSEL, STEAMSHIP COMPANY, OR OTHER MEANS OF TRANSPORTATION)

   ☆(c) I came as a (check one): Passenger..X..[1] Crew member..[2] Stowaway..[3] Other

   ☆(d) I entered the United States as a (check one): Permanent resident..X..[1] Visitor..[2] Student..[3]
   Treaty merchant..[4] Seaman..[5] Official of a foreign government..[6] Employee of a
   foreign government official..[7] Other

   ☆(e) I first arrived in the United States on .... Nov. 19 1909
   (MONTH) (DAY) (YEAR)

8. ☆(a) I have lived in the United States a total of ..... 31 .... years.

   ☆(b) I expect to remain in the United States .... permanently
   (PERMANENTLY, OR DURATION OF EXPECTED STAY)

9. (a) My usual occupation is Coach Cleaner (b) My present occupation is painter helper

   ☆(c) My employer (or registering parent or guardian) is A. T. S. F. Railway
   (NAME)

   whose address is .... Kansas City .... Kansas
   (STREET ADDRESS OR RURAL ROUTE) (CITY) (STATE)

   and whose business is .... transportation

All items must be answered by persons 14 years of age, or older. For children under 14 years of age, only the items marked with
a star (☆) must be answered by the parent or guardian. All answers must be accurate and complete.

Alien Registration Form- Pablo Dominguez

Baptism of Pablo Dominguez

ALIEN REGISTRATION RECORDS

As indicated by this document, Uncle Pablo was born on April 2, 1905, as he had stated in the alien registration form. He was baptized three days later at the small chapel of Rio de Medina in the municipio of Sain Alto, Zacatecas.

If you had a non-citizen ancestor in the United States who probably registered between 1940 and 1944, you should give serious thought to writing to the Immigration and Naturalization Service to see if they can locate relevant documents for you.

If you decide to write to the INS, you should obtain copies of *Freedom of Information Form OMB-1115-0087*. You can download this and other INS forms by visiting the following website:

http://www.ins.usdoj.gov/graphics/formsfee/forms/g-639.htm

However, you can also write directly to the INS Freedom of Information Office in Washington, D.C. for this information. You must state that you are making your request "under the provisions of the *Freedom of Information Act*" and you must give as much information as possible. If this person is recently deceased, it is recommended that you send a copy of his or her death certificate, an obituary, or some other proof of death, if possible. The address that you should write to in order to obtain Alien Registration records is as follows:

INS Freedom of Information
2nd Floor, ULLB
425 I Street, NW
Washington, D.C. 20536

Both alien registration and naturalization records are important sources of key information relating to your family history. It is through them that you will locate the time of arrival of your ancestor in the United States, the place of arrival, and the town of origin in Mexico. Once you have been fortified with this new information, it is possible for you to move towards the acquisition of key documents. Having acquired a date of immigration, you can seek out relevant border crossing documents for your ancestors. You are also in a position to begin searching for your family in the parish books and civil registries of Mexico.

Chapter 6
Crossing the Border
John Schmal

For Mexican-American genealogists, a large untapped resource is becoming rapidly available, thanks to the efforts of the Immigration and Naturalization Service and NARA. These great reserves of information waiting to be exploited are Mexican border-crossing records. One of the primary sources of information for this chapter is the NARA adaptation of Ms. Claire Prechtel-Kluskens' article "Mexican Border Crossing Records," which was originally published in the National Genealogical Society Newsletter.[1] This adaptation can be accessed at the following NARA website:

http://www.archives.gov/researh_room/genealogy/immigrant_arrivals/ mexican_border_crossings.html

With the passing of the Steerage Act of March 2, 1819, the United States Congress required that every American seaport would henceforth collect and maintain ship passenger lists. If your ancestors passed through the ports of New York, Philadelphia, Boston, New Orleans or other seaports on their way to America sometime between 1820 and 1957, you can obtain and search through National Archives records in the hopes of locating an arrival record.

Unfortunately, American officials along the Mexican border were not required to keep arrival records until early in the Twentieth Century. Following the Immigration Act of February 14, 1903, service officers began inspecting aliens – other than Mexicans – at border inspection points. An INS website, entitled "Early Immigrant Inspection Along the US/Mexican Border," discusses inspection policy and procedure along the Mexican border during these early years. This website may can be accessed at the following URL:

http://www.ins.usdoj.gov/graphics/aboutins/history/articles/MBTEXT2. htm

---

[1] *National Genealogical Society Newsletter*, Vol. 25, Nos. 3-5 (May-Oct. 1999): 156-157, 159, 182-183, 287-281.

CROSSING THE BORDER

The inspection of Mexican nationals along the Mexican ports of entry commenced on July 1, 1906. Many of these inspection records have been published on microfilm by NARA. If you wish to access the list of available microfilm publications for the twenty-four land border ports along the Mexican border from 1903 to 1952, you may want to return to the NARA site indicated earlier and read "Part 6: Available Microfilm Publications," which gives a detailed list of the microfilm collections available for certain ports and dates.

Part 7, which is entitled "Where to Find NARA Microfilm Publications," explains how you may view these films yourself. You can actually purchase a roll of microfilm by telephone for $34 dollars. However, it is important for you to consider the range of years and number of rolls of microfilm that make up a certain record group.

For example, M1757, Manifests of Aliens Granted Temporary Admission at El Paso, Texas, circa July 1924-1954, consists of ninety-seven rolls of film, which contain at least 245,000 alphabetically arranged manifests of people crossing the border. The NARA officials can help you to determine the range of surnames or years for a given roll of film within a record group.

In addition, you can visit NARA's regional facilities where the microfilms are also available for viewing in public reading rooms. The National Archives has provided us with the "NARA Archival Information Locator (NAIL)" which is designed to help you in this endeavor. This website can be accessed at:
http://www.archives.gov/research_room /nail/index.html

In order to give you – the reader – an appreciation of the content of these border-crossing records, we are including several of them in this chapter. On page 53, we have reproduced a copy of the ***List or Manifest of Alien Passengers for the United States Immigration Officer at Port of Arrival.*** Each individual tallied on this page by the border officer arrived at the El Paso port of entry on November 30 or December 1, 1906 and his or her information is carried across one line.

List or Manifest of Alien Passengers for the United States Immigration Officer at Port of Arrival

On Line 1 we see that on November 30, 1906, Felipe Guzman, 25 years of age, crossed the border. Moving from left to right on Line 1, we can see that Mr. Guzman was a single male laborer who was unable to read or write. His nationality was Mexican and his last permanent residence was in Pudal, Michoacan. He listed his final destination as El Paso. The second page of each manifest generally provides information about the physical description and destination of the passenger. We have not reproduced the second page here.

The second row of this document provides us with information relating to Segundo Chavez, whose last permanent residence was Las Bocas, Jalisco. It is important to note that these earliest manifests are woefully incomplete and that if you asked the National Archives to do a search for your Mexican ancestor who crossed the border in 1906 or 1907, you may not locate that person.

In 1908, the arrival manifests were replaced by card manifests, which consist of one full page of information about one individual. Service officers would complete a *Form 548* – also known as *Report of Inspection* – for each alien applying for admission at the ports of entry along the southern border. On page 55, you will see an example of the Report of Inspection for 38-year-old Anita Rodriguez, who crossed the border on September 17, 1908 at Eagle Pass, Texas.

Form 548 listed the personal description, place of birth, age, sex, marital status, occupation, last residence, and final destination of each passenger. In addition, the traveler was asked if he or she was a polygamist, anarchist, or had ever been in prison. In exploring this report, we find that Anita was born in Monclova, Mexico and left her last residence in Bajan, Mexico to visit her daughter in Texas.

On page 56, we have moved forward one decade to show you the manifest of another border-crosser. This document was recorded at the port of Tia Juana (Tijuana), California, on May 3, 1918 for a 38-year-old Mexican national named Maria Cruz de Reynoso. Although Maria had been born at San Miguel in the central state of Jalisco, her last residence was listed as Tijuana. She could neither read nor write.

Report of Inspection for Anita Rodriguez, who crossed the border on September 17, 1908 at Eagle Pass, Texas

● **MANIFEST** ●

U. S. DEPARTMENT OF LABOR

IMMIGRATION SERVICE

MEXICAN BORDER DISTRICT

Serial No. 1237

Serial 31

Record Sheet

Line 3

Port of Tia Juana, California.

(Dated) May 3, 1918.

Arrived via foot

PERSONAL DESCRIPTION

HEIGHT		COMPLEXION	COLOR OF		MARKS OF IDENTIFICATION	PLACE OF BIRTH
Feet	Inches		Hair	Eyes		
4	10	Med	Blk	Brn	Large scar under left ear Skin blotch between eyebrows	San Miguel, Jalisco, Mexico.

family, including daughter, Virginia, born in U.S.

Name Reynoso, Maria Cruz de   Accompanied by (8)   Sheet No. 31   Age 36

Sex F   Conjugal condition M   Occupation Housewife   Read No (Two w No)   Write No (Two w No)

Language or dialect read ———— Grounds for illiteracy exemption

Wife of admissible alien

Nationality Mexican   Race Mexican   Last residence Tijuana, B.C.Mexico

Final destination (d) Ray,Arizona   Ticket   Passage paid by Husband

Money No   Ever in U.S.? Yes   Period 1914-1916   Location California & Arizona,

Going to join Brother-in-law   Name and address { Gregorio Reynoso, Ray, Arizona.

Whether previously deported within one year, if so, and reapplication for admission has been authorized, give authority No

Health (c)   Whether in transit (f) No

Port of egress   Head tax assessed against (g) Yes   Receipt No. 15307   Exempt Par

Purpose in coming To reside

Whether intend return country whence came after laboring temporarily U. S. Yes

Length of time intend remain U. S. 2 years   Whether intend become citizen U. S. No

Action by primary inspector (h) Admitted

Sworn to before me this day.

Immigrant.*   Assessable.*

Nonstatistical. (f)

Nonimmigrant.*   Nonassessable.*

Inspector

Interpreter

CHARACTER OF HEAD-TAX CERTIFICATE (j)

Straight.*

Special deposit ("S. I.," "T.," "C.," "Temp.")   Refund ordered   ?

ACTION BY BOARD OF SPECIAL INQUIRY (2)   B. S. I. Serial No.

Admitted   ?   Deferred to   ?

Cause   Cause

Excluded   ?

Appeal taken by

DEPARTMENTAL ACTION

Decision   Final action   (Date)

Criminal Prosecution (m)   Witness (Sec 18) (n)

Complaint filed   ?   Final action   ?   Detained from   ? to

* Check appropriate heading   † Insert date

**Report of Inspection for Maria Cruz de Reynoso, Tia Juana
(Tijuana), California, on May 3, 1918**

CROSSING THE BORDER

When asked if she had ever been to the United States, Maria Cruz de Reynoso stated that she been in California and Arizona in 1914-1916. She told the border official that she was coming to the United States to reside for two years and that her final destination was the home of her brother-in-law, Gregorio Reynoso, in Ray, Arizona. Although the Immigration Act of 1917 had required aliens to pass a literacy test before crossing the border, Maria was granted an exemption from the literacy requirement because she was the "wife of [an] admissible alien."

Form 621 (Statistical) was another manifest used in the early years. On page 58, to show you can example of a statistical manifest, we have reproduced the border-crossing record for 47-year-old Concepcion Casas. Concepcion, traveling from Piedras Negras in Mexico to San Antonio, Texas, was admitted at the Eagle Pass port of entry on May 13, 1927.

The document states that Concepcion Casas was accompanied by her husband (Carlos Cadena) and three children and that they were planning to join her son, Homero Cadena. It is further noted that her passage was paid by the husband. Those who paid the head tax were tallied as statistical entries. Clearly, Form 621 has provided us with a great deal of information on a given individual, including health status, height, complexion, place of birth and destination.

Immigration and Naturalization officials have stated that, before 1930, aliens entering the U.S. from Mexico were usually not tallied if they planned to stay in the country for less than six months. Thus, if your ancestor entered the United States with the stated intention of working for a few months but decided to stay permanently, he may not have been tallied by border officials.

Starting around 1930, the INS developed forms and manifests to deal with short-term visitors to the United States. On page 59, we have reproduced a *Record of Alien Admitted as Visitor*. On April 26, 1943, 35-year-old Eduardo Drivet Mologra, a native of Guanajuato, was issued a visitor card. Although born in central Mexico, Eduardo, by this time, had moved north to Torreon, Coahuila, which he listed as his home address. The record also lists his physical characteristics and gives the name of his nearest relative in Mexico. This visitor card was issued for a five-day period ending on April 30, 1943.

N-Q-I-MEX.

Form 621   (STATISTICAL)

Manifest No. 6317

Name **Casas, Concepcion**   Age **47** Sex **F**

Conj. cond. **M**   Occupation **none**   Read **Yes**

W'd'w **Yes**   Illit. exempt **—**   Race **Mex.**

Last res. **Piedras Negras, Mex**   Class **i-s-str.**

Future res. **SAN ANTONIO, TEXAS**   Passage paid by **husb.**

Going to join **son: Homero Cadena.**   Money **none**

ADMITTED at **Eagle Pass, Texas**   Date **MAY 13 1927**

Med. Cert. **in good health**   S. I. No. **—**

Height **5'4"**   Complexion **Drk**   Hair **Blk-Gray** Eyes **Brn**

Marks **none.**

Place of birth **San Buenaventura, Coah Mex.**   Nationality **Mex.**

Accompanied by **Hus: Carlos Cadena, and 8 children.**

U. S. Department of Labor
Immigration Service

**Form 621, Statistical Manifest for Concepcion Casas admitted
at the Eagle Pass port of entry on May 13, 1927**

CROSSING THE BORDER

Form 5-C No. 152081 Iss. Torreon, Coah.,Mex.
I-186ß No. 1112383, valid to 4-16-44.
(2nd Form 5-7(a)) Iss N. Laredo.

U. S. DEPARTMENT OF JUSTICE MEMORANDUM COPY

IMMIGRATION AND NATURALIZATION SERVICE

RECORD OF ALIEN ADMITTED AS VISITOR

Port. EL PASO, TEXAS

Date 4-26-43   N⁰ 8752

8752

Name DRIVET Mologra, Eduardo

35 yrs,
Date and place of birth Guanajuato, Gto., Mexico

Nationality MEXICO   Race WHITE

Sex M Ht. 5' 7" Comp. Lt Hair Blk. Eyes Brn

My children, under 16 years, accompanying me, are None

Home address Torreon Coah., Mexico.

Nearest relative there Fath: Francisco Drivet,
Mother - Guanajuato, Gto, Mex.
Destined to El Paso, Tex.

Address El Paso, Texas, Tex.

Time for which admitted 5 days to 4-30-43, 3-2

Signature

Admitted by _____
                    U. S. Immigrant Inspector.

**Record of Alien Admitted as Visitor for Eduardo Drivet
Mologra, April 26, 1943**

CROSSING THE BORDER

Another document used for short-term border crossers was the ***Record of Alien Admitted for Temporary Stay***. On page 61, we have reproduced the document for one Isabel Dominguez de Morones, who was admitted to the United States on March 28, 1949. It appears that Isabel had left her home in Juarez, Chihuahua to visit her son-in-law, Dolores Olvera, in El Paso, Texas.

Isabel was born on June 2, 1888 in Torreon, Coahuila and apparently had not entered the United States before. The name of her closest relative (her husband, Cesareo Morones) was given, and two travel documents in the possession of the passenger were cited. The period of Isabel's intended stay was limited to 29 days.

On page 62, we have also reproduced the ***Application for Nonresident Alien's Border Crossing Identification Card*** of one Jesus Lopez-Morin. The applicant had been born in Parras, Coahuila on September 23, 1927, but lived in Ciudad Juarez at the time of this application. Jesus furnished his passport number, issued in 1951 by Mexican Migration, and stated that his purpose for coming to the United States was "to visit and make purchases."

One of the most common card manifests for border-crossers was the ***Form I-448, Manifest***. On pages 63 and 64, we have reproduced the very detailed I-448 Manifest that was filled out for Celia Acosta-Zaldivar on January 18, 1952. Celia was accompanied by her cousin, Maria Zaldivar, in her journey to America and claimed to be an American citizen who had lived in the United States from May 20, 1926 (her date of birth) to about 1943. She planned to visit the United States, but to continue to reside in Juarez, Chihuahua.

When Celia arrived at El Paso on this winter day in 1952 she came prepared with both documentation and a witness. On the backside of Celia's border-crossing record, we find a great deal of collateral information. Celia listed two of her children, who had been born in Los Angeles, California and baptized at Saint Anthony de Padua Church in the same city.

1	2	3	4	5	6	7	8	9	10	11	12

NAME   DOMINGUEZ de Morones, ISABEL   (a)   Nº 1288056

OCCUPATION   None

HOME ADDRESS   Callejon Carreno #219
Juarez, Chih., Mexico

ACCOMPANIED ALIEN CHILD UNDER 14
Dtr-Valentina Morones (15)
same documents.

DATE AND PLACE OF BIRTH 6-2-1888
Torreon, Coah., Mexico

M ☐   SX ☐   S ☐
F XX   W ☐   D ☐

HAIR   EYES   HEIGHT   NATIONALITY
Gry   Brn   5-0   Mexico

RACE
White

PURPOSE AND LENGTH OF INTENDED
STAY IN U. S.
3(2) "D" Pl-

MARKS
None noted.

DATE PREVIOUS ENTRY
Never

NAME AND ADDRESS OF NEAREST RELATIVE AT HOME
Husb-Cesareo Morones, same address.

29 days

DATE AND PLACE OF ADMISSION TO U. S.

2-28-49

El Paso, Texas

NAME AND ADDRESS OF PERSON TO WHOM DESTINED son-in-law.
Dolores Olvera, 3600 Alameda Ave., El Paso, Texas.

TRAVEL DOCUMENTS 67814 3-28-49 Juarez, Chih., Mexico
186 K12172 3-28-49 El Paso, Texas

MEANS OF TRANSPORTATION
EPCL Inc

DATE TO WHICH ADMITTED
April 25, 1949

U. S. IMMIGRANT INSPECTOR

RECORD OF ALIEN ADMITTED FOR TEMPORARY STAY

Form I-94 (a) (Rev 5-26-47)

Immigration and Naturalization Service, U. S. Department of Justice

8-9   14 50168-4

**Record of Alien Admitted for Temporary Stay for Isabel
Dominguez de Morones, 1949**

I, LOPEZ-Morin, JESUS

now residing at Cjon Honduras 318,Juarez,Chih.,Mexico hereby make application for a Border Crossing Identification Card and furnish the following information:

Born on 9-23-27 , at Parras,Coah.,Mexico

Sex Male Marital status single Occupation Cook
Read yes Write yes Nationality Mexico Height 5 ft. 2 in.
Weight 105 lb. Complexion Drk Hair Blk Eyes Brn
Visible distinctive marks or peculiarities None vis.
My passport is No. SC# 062260 Issued 6-2?-51 , by Mex.Mig.
Juarez,Chih.,Mexico valid to Indef.
My purpose in coming to United States is to visit & make purchases

**Application for Nonresident Alien's Border Crossing
Identification Card of Jesus Lopez-Morin**

Sworn MANIFEST	Arr. USC				
	Port of El Paso, Tex.	Date 1-18-52		Serial No.	
Family name ACOSTA-Zaldivar	Given name Celia			Accompanied by Cousin: Maria Z. LDIVA	

RAIG#441365,511½ So Oregon St. EPTex and Dtr: Olga CRUZ,

C.I.V.S. Place and date of issue None presented	Section and subdivisions Act of 1924:	Quota country charged	R.F.No. P.V.No.
Place of birth (town, country, etc.) 5-20-26 El Paso, Tex.	Age 25 Yrs Sex 7 Mos Female (M) S. W. D.	Occupation None	Read Yes Write
Language or exempt Spanish	Race White	Nationality Claims US	Last permanent residence (town, country, etc.) Gardenias#1208 Juarez Chih Mex.

Name and address of nearest relative or friend in country whence applicant came

Husb: Adolfo CRUZ, USC, same add.

Ever in U.S.A. From 5-20-26 Yes	To about 1943	Where EPTex.	Passage paid by Self

Destination and name and complete address of relative or friend to join there   in Juarez Chih Mex.

El Paso, Tex.temp., No one., To visit in US and continue to reside

Money shown None	Ever arrested and deported, or excluded from admission No		No	Purpose is contact and (something) to create record
Head tax status Ex USC	Height 5, 0	Complexion Dk.	Hair Blk	Eyes Brn	Distinguishing marks R/chin. Faint scrs: R/cheek &

Seaport etc. (something)   Cen. (or) identification card No.

Record:	Previously (something)	Date	Previous dest.	Present dispo: Adm USC	Arrived in EPCL Inc.
U.S.	DESTND DISTRICT				

Form I-448 First Page of Manifest for Celia Acosta-Zaldivar

DISPOSITION BEFORE B S I		VISITORS OR TRANSITS	
Deferred *or* and date	Rejected as and date	Visited 514 No.	Transit 514 or S. S. Line and Ticket No.

Date *approved*	Decision and date	Date *admitted*	File No.	Stampshing	Ticket *issued at and date*
4/25/52	USCM	15	772-85665		

MEDICAL CERTIFICATE

~~Affidavit with~~ ~~Children of CELIA ACOSTA-Zaldivar and Adolfo CRUZ by common~~
~~law marriage in Juares Chih Mex.(Both prin. are U.S.C.)~~
1. Jesus Adolfo CRUZ, born LACalif 8-30-44. Reg#19324. Bapt: Ch Sn
ant. de Padua, LA Calif 1-7-45.
2. Francisco CRUZ, LACailf 12-31-45; Reg#500, Bapt Ch SnAnt de Padua,
LACalif 2-24-46.

Surgeon, U. S. Public Health Service.

~~3. Olga CRUZ, Juares Chih Mex 5-9-51~~

REMARKS AND ENDORSEMENTS

Presents: birth cert showing Celia ACOSTA born to Jesus ACOSTA and
Rafaela ZALDIVAR at EPTex 5-20-26. Bapt Cert shows bapt at St. Ignati
us Ch,EPTex 8-1-26, Witness : Maria ZALDIVAR,RAIC#441365, 511½ So.
Oregon St. EPTex.,testified under oath that the appl is her cousin,
Celia; that celia was born EPTex 5-20-26; That her mother is my aunt.
that the appl is subj of certs presented.

Signature of applicant.

Immigrant Inspector

Second Page of Manifest for Celia Acosta-Zaldivar

CROSSING THE BORDER

Under Remarks and Endorsements, the immigration officer made note of documents that verified Celia's birth and baptism in El Paso. She had presented the INS official with a civil birth record, showing her date of birth (May 20, 1926). She also offered them a copy of her August 1, 1926 baptism certificate from St. Ignatius Church in El Paso. This large amount of detail is not uncommon in such manifests.

The Great Depression, commencing in 1929, led to a series of deportations and repatriations in the early 1930s that affected Mexican Americans in every part of the country. It is believed that more than a half million people were forced to leave the United States, and many of these forced migrants were actually American citizens by birth.

As a result of this action, the border-crossing manifests of the 1940s and 1950s show many American citizens returning to the U.S. after living for many years in Mexico. Some of these "returning citizens" may have been the victims of these forced exiles. On page 66 and 67, we have reproduced the sworn manifest of a "returning U.S. citizen" named Pedro Dorado-Flores.

Under "Remarks and Endorsements" on the backside of Pedro's card manifest, the immigration officer remarks that Pedro had presented him with a birth certificate from Fresno, indicating his California birth on January 31, 1931. There is also a reference to their departure (from the United States) on October 9, 1931 and his baptism in Jerez, Zacatecas on November 15, 1931, a month later. Additionally, a photo of Pedro is attached to the back of the card.

The expulsions of Mexican Americans reached their greatest height in 1931 and it is likely that Pedro's family may have been a part of this forced movement. In 1948, Pedro intended to come to the United States "to reside permanently" and to stay with his brother Ines Dorado in Saugus, California.

Sworn   Returning U S. citizen
MANIFEST   Port of El Paso, Texas   Date 9/13/48   Serial No.

Family name	Given name	Accompanied by
DORADO-Flores	Pedro	no one

C.I.V. No.	Place and date of issue	Section and subdivision	Quota country charged	U. No.
By U.S.		Act of 1924,		P.Z. No.

Place of birth (town, country, etc.)	Age	Yrs.	Mos.	Sex	M.	S.	Occupation	Read
Fresno, Calif	17		Mos.	M		WS D.	Farm Laborer	Write Yes

Language or exemption	Race	Nationality	Last permanent residence (town, country, etc.)
Spanish	white	U.S.	Jerez Zac. Mex.

Name and address of nearest relative or friend in country whence applicant came
Fa. Salvador Dorado   Calle de la Parroquia #115 Cd Garcia Zac.

Entered U.S. at	birth to 1931	Calif	Where	Passage paid by
Yes				self

Destination, and name and complete address of relative or friend to join there
Bro Inez Dorado Rt 1 Box 226 Saugus Calif

Money shown	Ever arrested and deported or excluded from admission	Purpose in coming and time of remaining
none	no	no	to reside Permanently

Head tax status	Height	Complexion	Hair	Eyes	Distinguishing marks
Ex U.S	5 Ft. 7 in.	dk	blk	brn	scar under rt jaw bone

Support and date of landing, and name of steamship
| | | | Cert. In Identification card No. |

Records by	Previously examined at	Date	Previous disposition	Present disposition, P.I.	Admitted by
					FULI

U. S. DEPARTMENT OF JUSTICE, Immigration and Naturalization Service   FORM I-448 (Ed. 1941)   8—13179
(Old 548)

First Page of Manifest for Pedro Dorado-Flores, 1948
Returning American Citizen

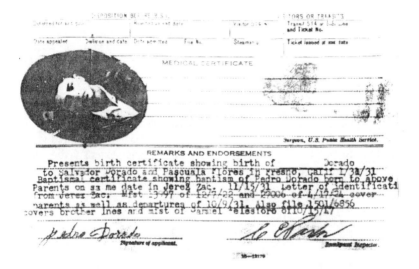

CROSSING THE BORDER

On page 69 and 70, we have reproduced the manifest for still another returning American citizen. In this case, 28-year-old Carmen Acosta Chavez, was crossing the border at El Paso on April 26, 1951. In this document, Carmen gives September 12, 1922 as her date of birth. Additionally, she tells the immigration officer that she was born in El Paso and lived in the U.S. from the time of her birth until March 24, 1931. Apparently she had resided in both Los Angeles, California and El Paso, Texas.

Listing Durango, Durango as her last residence, Carmen Acosta Chavez stated in this manifest that it was her intention to "resume residence" in her native land and that she would be staying with her brother, Carlos Acosta, a resident of El Paso. Under Remarks and Endorsements on the second page, the immigration officer testified that he had seen Carmen's birth record from El Paso, Texas.

The United States - Mexican border totals 1,951.36 official miles from the Gulf of Mexico to the Pacific Ocean. For more than a hundred years, millions of Mexican nationals have been crossing that extensive border to help alleviate the labor needs of the United States. In 1900, a total of 103,000 Mexican citizens lived within the boundaries of the United States. In 1910, this figure more than doubled to 222,000, and then doubled again to 478,000 by 1920.

By 1930, the number of Mexican-born residents of the U.S. had increased to more than 1,422,000. Most of these people crossed the border at the twenty-four ports of entry for which manifests are now available through the National Archives.

The development of a transportation system in northern Mexico that took place during the long rule of Porfirio Díaz (1876-1910) made possible this great movement of people. From a mere 400 miles in 1876 to 15,000 miles in 1910, Mexico's railway system became a major catalyst for the migration of Mexican northward into the United States. One of the most traveled routes was the Mexican Central Railway, which ran from Mexico City through Aguascalientes, Zacatecas, and Chihuahua to the border towns of Ciudad Juarez, Chihuahua, and El Paso, Texas.

Border-Crossing Record for Carmen Acosta Chavez, 1951

MEDICAL CERTIFICATE

Afflicted with

ALSO departure records show tht Carmen Acosta f, 7 yrs
Paso, Texas 9-3-23 last Resi in the US Los
Calif departed to Mex at this port on 3-24-31

Surgeon, U. S. Public Health Service.

REMARKS AND ENDORSEMENTS

PRESENTED Fe de B showing birth in El Paso, Texas 9-12-22 and Bap
ptism on 10-25-22; Birth Certif showing birth 9-13-22 at El Paso
Texas this certif put on record 9-20-22; departure records show
departure on 3-24-31; Old entry record show adm BSI on 1-3-22 with
4(c) visa. At that time birth was claimed at Santiago Papasquario
Dgo. mothers manifest 11226 of 1-3-28; Subj has sister Guadalupe
born Santiago Papasquario, Dgo. 12-13-40 who is liigi.

Carmen Acosta

**Border-Crossing Record for Carmen Acosta Chavez, 1951
2nd Page**

CROSSING THE BORDER

Initially, the first links to the Central Railroad were made at El Paso and Laredo in the last years of the Nineteenth Century. As a result, Texas became the primary recipient of the Mexican labor heading into the U.S. However, in April 1927, with the completion of the Southern Pacific of Mexico Railroad linking Guadalajara (Mexico's second largest city) with Nogales, Arizona, the dynamics of the northward migration were changed significantly.[2]

Up until 1927, existing railway lines had forced most immigrants from Guadalajara and the populous state of Jalisco to enter the U.S. by way of El Paso. Now, however, an immediate influx of immigrants from Jalisco were able to make their way north to work in California and Arizona via Nogales.[3]

If your ancestors came from Mexico in the first half of the Nineteenth Century, it is possible that you may be able to locate detailed documentation for them. Finding and analyzing border-crossing, naturalization and alien registration records may help you to construct your family's paper trail to Mexico.

---

[2] Mark Reisler, *By The Sweat of Their Brow: Mexican Immigrant Labor in the United States, 1900 - 1940* (Westport, Connecticut: Greenwood Press, 1976), p. 26; "New S.P. de M.R.R. Open to Traffic," ***Nogales International***, April 17, 1927.
[3] *Ibid.*

Chapter 7
Best Records in the World
John Schmal

Many people look to Mexico as a nation rich in mineral resources, cultural antiquities and historical significance. Indeed, it is this... and much more. To the family history researcher, Mexico is a land whose vital records are rich in both detail and availability. Mexico's *Registros Parroquiales* (Parish Registers) – in particular – have provided many Mexican Americans with a fabulous window into their past.

From one end of Mexico to another, countless church books and civil registries have chronicled the life events of ordinary laborers and slaves, alongside those of wealthy landowners. Millions of baptisms, marriages and confirmations were performed and it appears that a great number of these church records have survived to the present day. Mexico's civil registration, enacted in 1859, provides the researcher with a secondary source that is sometimes even more detailed than the church records.

To help you better appreciate this valuable resource, we shall show you several documents from the Mexico of yesteryear. On page 75, we have reproduced the 1903 marriage record of Donna's paternal grandparents, Olayo Morales and Juana Luevano. This marriage record was performed by the Judge of the Civil Court in the small town of Cieneguilla in the state of Aguascalientes in central Mexico. The civil registry of birth, marriage and death records from Cieneguilla have been microfilmed by the Genealogical Society of Utah and are now available on seventeen rolls of film that are available through the Family History Library. This very detailed document has been translated into English as follows:[1]

---

[1] The Cieneguilla civil marriage records from 1903 are located on Microfilm 0299094 (Salt Lake City: Family History Library, 1987).

In Cieneguilla on January 18, 1903 at nine in the morning in this office and before the recording judge, appeared the citizens OLAYO MORALES and JUANA LUEVANO, who stated that they desired to be married (in a civil ceremony) in conformity with the applicable laws for which they will make their best efforts. The first party (Olayo) is single, 22 years of age, originally from Santa Maria and a resident of this place, a laborer, and the legitimate son of Eustacio Morales and Juana Salas, who are living.

The second party (Juana) is 16 years old, the legitimate daughter of Tiburcio Luevano and Manuela Martinez, who are also alive. At once, and at the end of the demonstration of their legal capacity to marry, introduced as witnesses were the citizens Crispin Santana (50 years of age) and Zacarias Salinas (60 years of age), both married and adults of age, laborers and residents of this hacienda, witnesses for the first party. The second party presented as witnesses the citizens Juan Perez and Eligio Chavez, both married, adults of age, laborers, and residents of this property, who under the protest of their truthfulness, declared that they are not aware of any impediments to marriage, prior to the consent of the parents, I, the Judge, made the presentation and I decided that it will be published for the period required by law. According to the content that was read to the people present in front of me, I, the Judge, signed it. The people present did not sign it because they do not know how to write.

Signed, Pablo Valdivia

Marriage Record of Olayo Morales and Juana Luevano
Cieneguilla, Aguascalientes, 1903

The Genealogical Society of Utah also filmed the Parish Registers for the City of Aguascalientes in 1961. Starting in 1616 and continuing through 1961, the church files have been stored on 458 rolls of film and represent a fabulous collection of detailed religious events. [2] On page 77, we will go back to a marriage that was performed 115 years earlier to find the actual marriage certificate for the 1788 marriage of Jose Cipriano Gomes and Manuela Masias, Donna's great-great-great-great-grandparents. As you can see, this document contains many abbreviated words. In many parts of Mexico, the Spanish padres made use of abbreviations as a means of saving both ink and paper, which, in those days, were scarce commodities. This marriage record is translated as follows: [3]

In the Village of Aguas Calientes on the 23rd day of April, 1788, having presided over the usual preparatory steps and having read the arranged marriage banns as required by the Holy Council of Trent in the parish church on three holy days in solemn Mass on the 6th, 13th, and 20th days of the current month, and no impediment to marriage having resulted, I, Father Sir Thomas Serrano, with permission from Father Andres Martinez, the senior interim parish priest, assisted in the marriage in my presence and by these words celebrated in Holy Mass – JOSE CIPRIANO GOMES, Spanish, originally from and a resident of this jurisdiction in Juiquinaqui, legitimate son of Antonio Gomes and Rita Quitaria de Robalcava – and MANUELA MASIAS, Spanish, originally from this jurisdiction in the Canutillo and resident of the above-mentioned Juiquinaqui, natural daughter of Ines Masias (deceased) – (were joined) in Blessed Nuptials. The godparents were Antonio Flores and Dolores Garcia and witnesses, Matias Hernandez and Juan Valades – In witness thereof we signed it.

---

[2] Copyright © 1999 by the Intellectual Reserve, Inc.
[3] The Aguascalientes marriage records of 1788 are found on Microfilm 0299832 (Salt Lake City: Genealogical Society of Utah, 1961).

**Marriage Record of Jose Cipriano Gomes & Manuela Masias
Aguascalientes, 1788**

Both of the participants in this marriage, Jose Cipriano Gomes and Manuela Masias, were described by the priest as being "Spanish." This designation, however, does not mean that the bride and groom were actually born in Spain. Instead, it simply implies that the parish priest, upon observing both individuals, believed that they appeared to be of White descent, most likely Spanish.

Throughout colonial Latin America, the Spanish clerics were very diligent in their ethnological classifications. By the Sixteenth Century, the Spanish Government had created a variety of race categories that they used to identity persons of mixed ancestry and establish legal and social distinctions that would form the basis for their hierarchical colonial caste system. Frequently, these racial classifications were based primarily on the perception of the parish priest, who sometimes made stereotypical assumptions based on appearance, culture, behavior, and other factors.[4]

A few of the racial designations that were used in colonial Mexico are reproduced as follows:[5]

Designation	*Definition*
Español	Spanish
Indio	Indian
Negro	Black/African
Mestizo	Half Spanish / half Indian
Mulato	Half Spanish / half African
Zambo	Half Indian / half African
Lobo	African (3 parts) / Spanish (1 part)
Morisco	African (1 part) / Spanish (3 parts)
Coyote	African (2 parts) / Spanish (1 part) / Indian (1 part)
Cambuto	Spanish (3 parts) / African (1 part)
Jabaro	Spanish (1 part) Indian (6 parts) / African (1 part)

---

[4]   Robert H. Jackson, *Race, Caste, and Status: Indians in Colonial Spanish America* (Albuquerque, New Mexico: University of New Mexico Press, 1999), p. 4.
[5]   These racial classifications are discussed in more detail in Robert H. Jackson's *Race, Caste, and Status: Indians in Colonial Spanish* America. A full list of the 22 designations can be seen in *Spanish Records Extraction* (Salt Lake City: The Church of Jesus Christ of Latter-Day Saints, 1986), p. D-1.

As an example of a mixed marriage, we have reproduced on page 80 a 1774 marriage record from Charcas, San Luis Potosí, which indicates the marriage between one Jacinto Ramon Rodriguez Flores, a *mulato esclavo (slave mulato)*, and Maria Manuela Sauzeda (a *mestiza* from El Rancho del Sitio). The translation of this 228-year-old marriage document reads in part:[6]

> *In this Parish Church of Our Lady of Charcas on the 16th of August in 1774, having presided over the usual preparatory steps as required by the Holy Council of Trent and the synod of this town,... I married JACINTO RAMON RODRIGUEZ FLORES, a mulato, originally of Aalosto, servant in this place, widower of Rita Quiteria Felicia, who was buried in the Parish a year and three months ago, legitimate son of Francisco Rodriguez and Maria Magdalena Perez, deceased mulata slave,*
>
> *And MARIA MANUELA SAUZEDA, a mestiza of the Post of Animas in this jurisdiction and resident of Ranch of San Jose de Sitio, legitimate daughter of Francisco Xavier Zauzeda and Martina Xaviera Perez, and not having found any impediments, I proclaimed the banns of marriage...*

It appears that Jacinto was a widower who had lost his first wife a year and three months earlier. Mixed marriages of couples who had various combinations of Spanish, African, and Indian blood were common throughout Mexico. And, more amazingly, baptisms and marriages of many of these slaves were recorded by the Catholic priests in their local parish archives.

---

[6] The parish registers of San Francisco Church in Charcas range from 1586 to 1965 and are contained on a total of 211 rolls of film. The marriages performed in Charcas during 1774 are contained on Microfilm 707775.

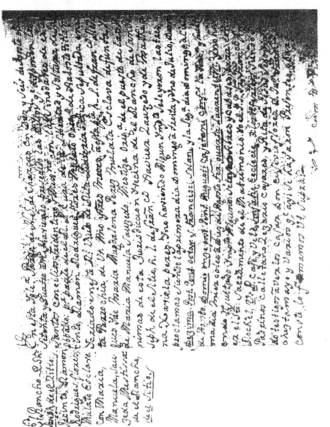

**Marriage Record of Jacinto Ramon Rodriguez Flores and
Maria Manuela Sauzeda, 1774**

In addition to the racial classifications, some colonial parishes actually kept separate baptismal and marriage books for Spaniards and persons of mixed ancestry. On page 82, we have reproduced the title page of one of the baptism books from the Aguascalientes Parish. The page can be roughly translated as follows: [7]

> ***Book in which reside the documents of the baptisms of Mulatos, Blacks, Indians, Coyotes, Mestizos, and Lobos, which took place in the Parish of the Village of the Assumption of the Our Lady of Aguascalientes. Residing priest in ownership: Doctor and Master Juan Carlos de Casafola, and his deputies, the bachelors Joseph de Mendoza and Vicente Preciado de Lizalde, and which commence in August 1717.***

On page 83, we present another title page from the Aguascalientes parish registry, which can be translated as follows: [8]

> ***Book 35 in which reside the documents of baptisms of Spaniards, separated from the rest of the other grades (of people); Residing priest in charge of this Village of Aguas Calientes: Señor Doctor Jose Antonio Acosta; I began on the 27th day of September in 1801.***

On page 84, we have reproduced the 1673 marriage record of Francisco de Cardona and Luisa de Robalcaba, who were married in Lagos de Moreno in the northern section of the state of Jalisco.

The parish records of Lagos de Moreno – which was known as Santa María de los Lagos until the Nineteenth Century – extend more than three hundred years into the past. If you visit the Family History Library catalog website, you will see that the Library itself has 476 rolls of film – ranging from 1634 to 1957 – which contain baptisms, confirmations,

---

[7] The title page for the Aguascalientes Baptism Book, dated 1717, is located on Microfilm 0299425 (Salt Lake City: Genealogical Society of Utah, 1961).

[8] The title page for the Aguascalientes Baptism Book, dated 1801, is located on Microfilm 0299457 (Salt Lake City: Genealogical Society of Utah, 1961).

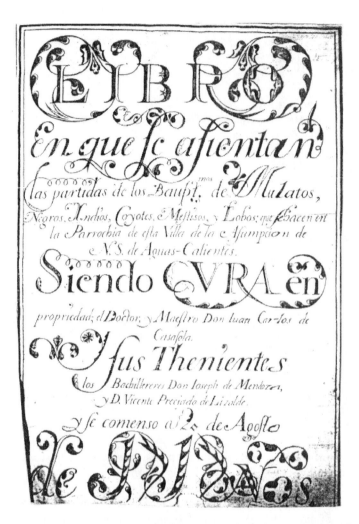

**Aguascalientes Parish Title Page, 1717, Showing Baptisms of
Mixed-Raced Children**

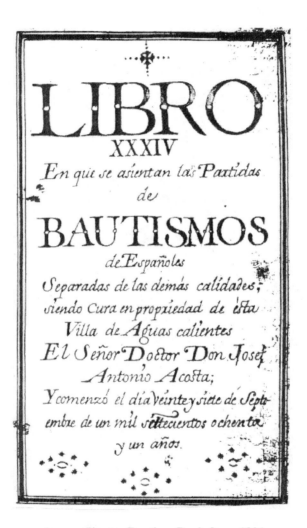

Aguascalientes Baptism Book from 1801
Showing Spanish Baptisms

Marriage of Francisco de Cardona and Luisa de Robalcaba
Lagos de Moreno, Jalisco, 1673

marriage petitions, marriages and death from Lagos de Moreno. The marriage record of Francisco de Cardona and Luisa de Robalcaba, has been translated as follows: [9]

> *On the 6th day of the month of July of the year 1673, I married and veiled within the church FRANCISCO DE CARDONA, a native of Saint Bartholome de la Agua, a dependent of the Bishopric of Guadalajara (licensed as a legitimate parish), legitimate son of Francisco de Cardona and Magdalena de Carbajal,*
>
> *With LUISA DE ROBALCABA, native of this village, legitimate daughter of Jose Gonsalez de Robalcaba and Ana Gonsalez Florida (already deceased), resident of this village, having presided over the conciliar measures as required by the Holy Council of Trent, and having published the marriage banns in Holy Mass on three holy days, on Sunday the 9th of July, Sunday the 16th of July and Saturday the 22nd of July. I continued (with the marriage), no impediments to marriage that I know of having resulted...*

One of the most prized possessions of the family history researcher of Mexican records is the document which will give him new clues and lead him to new horizons of research. In the Mexico of former centuries, some people moved from one place to another. This was especially the case in a frontier area like the state of Chihuahua in northern Mexico.

In 1958, the Genealogical Society of Utah filmed the parish registers of Hidalgo de Parral – now in the state of Chihuahua – and placed their documents of marriage and baptism on a total of forty rolls of film. These registers range from 1632 to 1958 and are available for viewing through the Family History Library. One of the more interesting documents I have located in this collection is the 1706 marriage record of

---

[9] The marriages of 1673 for Lagos de Moreno are contained on Microfilm 0221404 (Salt Lake City: Genealogical Society of Utah, 1958).

Juan Bernardo Perchez and Josepha Franco. This document, which has been reproduced on page 87, has been partially translated as follows: [10]

> *On the Fourth of May of 1706, in the house of the dwelling of Lorenzo de Aguirre, a Spanish resident and merchant of this place of Parral, the licensee Antonio Lopez, priest, with my permission, married through the present words, according to Our Holy Mother Church, JUAN BERNARDO DE PERCHEZ, native of Loches in the Archbishopric of Toares in the Kingdom of France, the legitimate son of Bernardo de Perchez and of Maria Luisa, residents of the said city....*
>
> *And JOSEFA FRANCO, native of the village of Madrid in the Kingdom of Castilla, legitimate daughter of Martin Franco and Josefa Cortez, residents of the said village...*

This document – in addition to telling us about the marriage of a young couple in the early Eighteenth Century – has told us that the groom was born in the Kingdom of France, while the bride was a native of Madrid in the Kingdom of Castilla (now Spain).

In the early parish archives of Aguascalientes, we found a similar document for the marriage of Donna Morales' great-great-great-great-great-great-great-great-grandparents, Luis Tiscareno de Molina and Lorenza Ruiz de Esparza. We have decided not to reproduce this marriage record as some parts of the document are not readable. However, the marriage document, dated May 16, 1623, makes reference to the groom, Luis Tiscareno de Molina, who is described as the son of Juan Tiscareno and Elvira Marquez. They are listed as *"naturales de Triana en Sevilla Reynos de Castilla"* (natives of Triana in Sevilla, the Kingdom of Castile, in Spain).

---

[10] This marriage document has been made available through the courtesy of Jaime Pacheco. The marriage records of Hidalgo de Parral, Chihuahua for the year 1706 are contained on Microfilm 162555 (Salt Lake City: Genealogical Society of Utah, 1958).

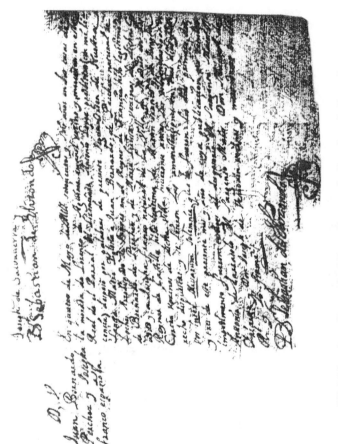

1706 Marriage Record of Juan Bernardo Perchez & Josepha Franco, Hidalgo de Parral, Chihuahua

Having discussed two documents that bridge the Atlantic Ocean between Mexico and Europe, we are given a new appreciation of the multidimensional nature of Mexico's cultural and genetic roots. As you – the reader – can see, the detail found in civil and church records for many cities and towns of Mexico can be most revealing. This level of detail cannot be found in the church records of many other countries.

As we conclude this chapter, you are probably asking yourself "These documents are so impressive. If I have located the towns from which my ancestors came, can I find out how to access these parish registers?" The answer to your question is pretty simple: "Yes." As indicated in an earlier chapter, you can access the Family History Library Catalog at *http://www.familysearch.org/Eng/Library/FHLC/frameset_fhlc.asp*. From this point, you can utilize the *Place Search*. When you enter the name of your ancestral city or town, you should get a presentation of the records available through the library.

If, however, you do not get any results, we recommend that you purchase a large-scale map of the state you are dealing with and try to locate the hacienda, pueblo or villa on this kind of map. Most atlases and tourist brochures for Mexico only show the largest and most historically significant cities. Your place of origin may only show up on the largest, most detailed maps, which you can probably purchase through *Amazon.com*.

If you have access to a Gazetteer for Mexico, you may obtain similar results by pinpointing the geographic coordinates of the location and then trying to locate them on a map.

As one example of a printout from the Family History Library Catalog, we have reproduced on page 89 and 90 the display for the Catholic Church records of Sombrerete, Zacatecas.[11] As you can clearly see, the records from Sombrerete start in 1678 and are available up to 1940 on forty-two rolls of microfilm. The Genealogical Society of Utah microfilmed most of these documents in 1966 and 1994.

---

[11] Reprinted by permission. Copyright © 1999 by the Intellectual Reserve, Inc.

THE BEST RECORDS IN THE WORLD

AUTHOR
Iglesia Católica. San Juan Bautista (Sombrerete, Zacatecas).

TITLE
Registros parroquiales, 1678-1940.

PUBLICATION INFORMATION
Salt Lake City : Filmados por la Sociedad Genealógica de Utah, 1966, 1994.

FORMAT
42 carretes de microfilme ; 35 mm.

NOTES
Microfilme de manuscritos en el archivo parroquial.

CONTENTS
Parish registers of baptisms, confirmations, marriages, marriage
petitions, deaths, and other church records from Sombrerete,
Zacatecas, Mexico.
Many of the registers include an index.
Muchos de los registros incluyen índice.

		LATIN AMERICA FILM AREA
Bautismos	1679-1688, 1693-1695, ----------	0604811
1710-1770		
Bautismos	1741-1747, 1758-1760 ----------	0604812
Bautismos	1761-1777 --------------------	0604813
Bautismos	1789-1791, 1794-1795, ----------	0604814
1797-1800		
Bautismos	1802-1803, 1809-1825 ----------	0604815
Bautismos	1824-1825, 1833, --------------	0604816
1839-1841		
Bautismos	1863-1869 --------------------	0604817
Bautismos	1865-1869 --------------------	0604818
Bautismos	1869-1871 --------------------	0604819
Bautismos	1871-1880 --------------------	0617424
Bautismos	1872-1878 --------------------	0654972
Bautismos	1876-1879 --------------------	0654973
Bautismos	1878-1889 --------------------	0654974
Bautismos	1881-1886 --------------------	0654975
Bautismos	1886-1890 --------------------	0654976
Bautismos	1889-1893 --------------------	0654977
Bautismos	1893-1896 --------------------	0654978
Bautismos	1896-1899 --------------------	0654979
Bautismos	1899-1901 --------------------	0654980
Confirmaciones	1869-1903 --------------------	0654981
Matrimonios	1695-1788 --------------------	0654982
Matrimonios	1793-1854 .-------------------	0654983
Información matrimonial	1863-1878 --------------------	0654984
Información matrimonial	1867-1889 --------------------	0654985
Información matrimonial	1890-1900 --------------------	0654986
Información matrimonial	1891-1892 --------------------	0654987
Información matrimonial	1892-1896 --------------------	0654988
Información matrimonial	1896-1899 --------------------	0654989
		item 1

Sombrerete Printout Page 1

THE BEST RECORDS IN THE WORLD

```
Docmentos eclesiásticos      1895-1920 --------------------- 0654989
                                                             item 2.
Defunciones                  1678-1811 --------------------- 0654990
Defunciones                  1809-1901 --------------------- 0654991
Bautismos    ℓ. 41-46        1902-1904 --------------------- 1909685
Bautismos    ℓ. 47-53        1904-1908 --------------------- 1909686
Bautismos    ℓ. 54-59        1908-1912 --------------------- 1909687
Bautismos    ℓ. 60-65        1912-1915 --------------------- 1909688
Bautismos    ℓ. 66-70        1915-1922 --------------------- 1909689
Bautismos    ℓ. 71-74        1922-1927, 1929 -------------- 1909690
Bautismos    ℓ. 74-77        1929-1931 --------------------- 1909691
Confirmaciones    ℓ. 6-7     1910-1914, 1919-1931 --------- 1909692
   (El ℓ. 6 incluye algunas de la parroquia de              item 1-2
   Fresnillo.)
Matrimonios  ℓ. 19-28        1901-1911 --------------------- 1909692
   (Falta el ℓ. 23.)                                        item 3-11.
Matrimonios  ℓ. 29-36   1911-1914 ----------------------- 1909693
   (Incluyen informaciones matrimoniales.)
Matrimonios  ℓ. 36-43 bis 1914-1925 --------------------- 1909694
   (Los ℓ. 37-41 incluyen informaciones
   matrimoniales y el ℓ. 42 incluye dispensas.)
Matrimonios  ℓ. 43 bis-44 1925-1926, 1929-1931 ---------- 1909695
                                                             item 1-2
Noticias matrimoniales   ℓ. 1        1908-1940 ----------- 1909695
   (Faltan años.)                                            item 3
Informaciones matrimoniales ℓ. 1-3 1915-1922 ----------- 1909695
                                                             item 4-6
Presentaciones matrimoniales ℓ. 2-3 1922-1924 ---------- 1909695
                                                             item 7-8.
Presentaciones matrimoniales ℓ. 4    1924 --------------- 1909696
                                                             item 1
Informaciones matrimoniales   ℓ. 4-6 1924-1926, --------- 1909696
   1929-1931                                                 item 2-4
Entierros    ℓ. 2-4          1901-1940 --------------------- 1909696
                                                             item 5-7.
```

THIS RECORD FOUND UNDER
   1. Mexico, Zacatecas, Sombrerete - Church records

Sombrerete Printout Page 2

THE BEST RECORDS IN THE WORLD

If you are interested in taking a look at this film, you will be able to visit any Family History Center in this country and order any one roll of microfilm for $3.77. For this small fee, a roll of film will be sent from the library in Salt Lake City to your Family History Center for a period of a month. For you this may be the beginning of a great journey that will take your family history research back three centuries.

The forty-two rolls of film that contain the Sombrerete parish records are just one example for you to consider. The Family History Library owns 152,600 rolls of film for all of Mexico. This huge collection of film is, at the moment, an untapped reservoir of family history information waiting to be discovered and studied by Mexican Americans who are eager to learn more about their ancestor's lives.

Chapter 8
Passengers to the Indies
John Schmal

At some point in the family history research for your Mexican ancestors, it is likely that you will find that some of your forbearers came from Europe. Many people have asked me how they may find out about their ancestors who traveled from Spain to Mexico at some point in the past. As you might expect, you cannot hope to locate any ancestors in Spain until you first locate your family in Mexico and research them as far back into the past as you possibly can.

But, once you have traced your ancestors back several generations, you may be able to locate a document – similar to the last two marriage documents discussed in the last chapter – which will lead you back to Europe. Sometimes, the death records of certain persons in Mexico may state that the decedent was born in some part of Spain. But there are other sources of information too. There are published compilations of passenger lists for the Spanish people who crossed the Atlantic Ocean to the West Indies and other parts of Latin America in earlier centuries. The best indexed source for Spanish emigration to Latin America – including Mexico – is the *Catalogo de Pasajeros a Indias Durante Los Siglos XVI, XVII y XVIII* (Catalog of the Passengers to the Indies During the Fifteenth, Sixteenth and Seventeenth Centuries).

The passenger lists of the voyagers who traveled from Spain to the Western Hemisphere during the Sixteenth, Seventeenth, and Eighteenth Centuries have been compiled at various times since the 1930s, and some have been microfilmed by the Family History Library. Volumes I (1509-1533), Volume II (1535-1538), and Volume III (1539-1559) were compiled and edited under the direction of Cristobal Bermudez Plata and published by the Archivo General de las Indias. The Family History Library has published two copies of each of these volumes.[1]

---

[1] Copyright © 2000 by the Intellectual Reserve, Inc. Volumes I and II of *Catalogo de Pasajeros* can be found on Microfilms 0277577 and 1410933. Volume III can be found on Microfilms 0277578 and 1410934.

Volume IV (1560-1566) and Volume V (1567-1577) were compiled by Luis Romera Iruela and Maria del Carmen Galbis Diez and published by Spain's *Ministerio de Cultura* in 1980. Volume VI (1578-1585) and Volume VII (1586-1599) were compiled by María del Carmen Galbis Diez and also published by Spain's Ministerio de Cultura in 1986. All the volumes – from I through VII – have been indexed by surname and location.

As an example of the entries one will find in these volumes, Volume III has an entry for one Alonso de Torres who left Spain in 1540. Listed as Entry #501, this passage reads as follows:[2]

> *Alonso de Torres, hijo de Juan de Albadán y de Catalina de Villalobos, vecinos de Sevilla, a Nueva España – 7 Abril.*

Translated from Spanish into English, this entry means: "Alonso de Torres, son of Juan de Albadán and of Catalina de Villalobos, residents of Seville, to New Spain – on April 7." Nueva España was the Spanish colonial name for Mexico. There are some entries in *Catalogo de Pasajeros* which are more detailed than the last one. For example, another entry from the same date reads as follows:[3]

> *Francisco Rodríguez, hijo de Juan López y de Florentina Rodríguez, vecinos de Sevilla, a Nueva España con su mujer Juana Sánchez, y sus hijos Diego Sánchez, Antonio de Paula, Florentina Rodríguez, Brígida Rodríguez y Francisco Rodríguez – 7 Abril.*

Translated into the English language, this entry reads as follows: "Francisco Rodriguez, son of Juan Lopez and of Florentina Rodriguez, residents of Seville, to New Spain, with his woman (wife), Juana Sanchez, and his children..." An entry such as this, in addition to providing a place of origin in Spain, actually provides the names for three generations of this family: Francisco Rodriguez and his wife, his

---

[2] Cristobal Bermudez Plata, *Catalogo Pasajeros a Indias Durante Los Siglos XVI, XVII y XVIII: Volumen III (1539-1559)*, (Sevilla, Spain: Imprenta de al Gavidia, 1946), Año 1540, p. 95.

[3] Ibid.

parents, and his five children. These entries are not uncommon and may bring about a great breakthrough in one's family history research.

So far, we have been able to locate one confirmed **Pasajeros** ancestor for Donna Morales. An entry from 1593 in Volume VII reads as follows: [4]

> *Lope Ruiz de Esparza, natural de Pamplona, soltero,*
> *hijo de Lope Ruiz de Esparza y de Ana Díaz de*
> *Eguino, a Nueva España como criador de don*
> *Enrique de Maleón. – 8 febrero.*

Translated into English, this entry reads "Lope Ruiz de Esparza, native of Pamplona, single, son of Lope Ruiz de Esparza and Ana Diaz de Eguino, to New Spain, as servant of Don Enriguez de Maleon on February 8, 1593." Pamplona is the largest city of the northern Spanish province of Navarre.

We have accumulated evidence that Lopez Ruiz de Esparza first arrived in Mexico City and later moved on to Aguascalientes, where his descendants live to this day. As a matter of fact, he is the father of Lorenza Ruiz de Esparza, who was mentioned in the 1623 marriage record in Chapter 7.

Compiled passenger lists of emigration from Spain to her American colonies for 1600 to 1701 are presently in the hands of Archivo de las Indias. Although these future volumes of **Catalogo de Pasajeros** have not been published yet, they are available for consultation in the study rooms of the Archivo de Indias in Seville, Spain.

You can access more detailed information about **Pasajeros a Indias** by visiting the following URL: ***http://www.cubagenweb.org/pass.htm.*** According to this website, the **Archivo General de Indias** is in the process of preparing a CD-ROM containing most of the data that has not already been published. However, no date of publication has been specified at the present time. The URL of the **Archivo General** in Sevilla can be accessed at ***http://www.mcu.es/lab/archivos/AGI.html.***

---

[4]Maria del Carmen Galbis Diez, **Catalogo Pasajeros a Indias Durante Los Siglos XVI, XVII y XVIII**: **Volumen VII (1586-1599)**, (Spain: Ministerio de Cultura, 1986), Año 1593, p. 384.

Chapter 9
The Indians of Mexico
John Schmal

Across the 756,066 square miles that comprise Mexico you can find a great variety of landscapes and climates. While mountains and plateaus cover more than two-thirds of her landmass, the rest of Mexico's environment is made up of deserts, tropical forests, and fertile valleys. Mexico's many mountain ranges tend to split the country into countless smaller valleys, each forming a world of its own.

Mexico's "fragmentation into countless mountain valleys, each with its own mini-ecology," according to the historian Nigel Davies, led the Indians within each geographical unit to develop their own language and culture.[1] This cultural development is a key to understanding Mexican history. Mexico's remarkable cultural and linguistic diversity, in large part, led to her conquest by the Spaniards. Speaking as many as 300 mutually alien languages and dialects, most of the Mexican Indians viewed each other with great suspicion from the earliest times.

When Hernán Cortés (1485-1547) came to Mexico in 1519, he found a large but fragmented collection of tribes, some of which were at war with each other. It was this dissension and lack of unity that he exploited to his advantage. Even today, almost five centuries after *The Conquest*, the indigenous peoples of Mexico speak 288 languages.[2]

To give you, the reader, an appreciation of the diversity of cultures found in one part of Mexico, we have reproduced on page 98, a map showing the distribution of the native languages in the west central portion of Mexico.[3]

---

[1] Nigel Davies, *The Ancient Kingdoms of Mexico* (London: Penguin Books, 1990), p. 15.

[2] Source: Online: http://www.ethnologue.com/show_country.asp?name=Mexico (April 10, 2002) from Barbara F. Grimes (ed.), "Ethnologue: Languages of the World" (14th edition). Dallas, Texas: SIL International, 2001.

[3] Eric Van Young, "The Indigenous Peoples of Western Mexico From the Spanish Invasion to the Present," in Richard E.W. Adams and Murdo J. MacLeod, *The Cambridge History of the Native Peoples of the Americas: Volume II, Mesoamerica, Part 2* (Cambridge, UK: Cambridge University Press, 2000), Map 15.2, p. 144.

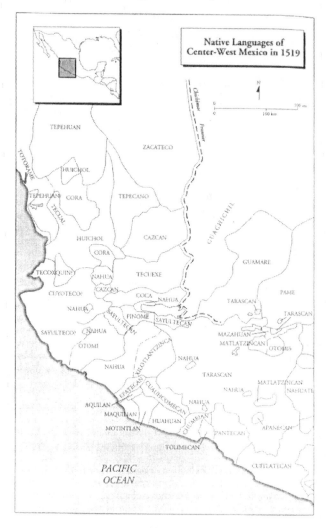

Map 15.2

Map of Center West Mexico, Cambridge University

THE INDIANS OF MEXICO

Other sections of Mexico are no less complex and – in some cases – much more diversified.

We believe that at least three-quarters of Donna's ancestors were classified as Indians or mestizos. The majority of these Indian and mestizo ancestors lived in what we now call Jalisco and Zacatecas, two central states of Mexico. The Indians of these regions were collectively called the **Chichimecas**, a derogatory epithet given to them by the Aztec Indians, who were themselves of Chichimec descent. It is from this large Indian group – now culturally extinct – that many Mexican Americans descend.

The definitive source for information relating to the Chichimeca Indians is Philip Wayne Powell's **Soldiers, Indians, and Silver: North America's First Frontier War**.[4] On page 100, is a map, reproduced from J. Lloyd Mecham's **Francisco de Ibarra and Nueva Vizcaya**, that indicates the approximate boundaries of the various Chichimec nations in 1550.[5] The present-day states of Zacatecas, Guanajuato, Aguascalientes, Queretaro, Durango, Nayarit and Jalisco occupy most of this territory today.

We believe that the Chichimeca Indians and their fifty-year resistance to Spanish rule (1550-1600) is significant because the aftermath of that conflict (known as **La Guerra de los Chichimecas – The War of the Chichimecas**) is archetypal of what was repeated many times in other parts of Mexico. The Chichimeca conflict and other wars of resistance forced the Spaniards to rely heavily upon their Christian Indian allies. The result of this dependence upon indigenous allies as **soldados** (soldiers) and **pobladores** (settlers) led to enormous and wide-ranging migration and resettlement patterns that would transform the geographic nature of the peoples of Mexico.

---

[4] Philip Wayne Powell's *Soldiers, Indians and Silver: North America's First Frontier War* (Tempe, Arizona: Center for Latin American Studies, Arizona State University, 1975).
[5] J. Lloyd Mecham, *Francisco de Ibarra and Nueva Vizcaya* (Durham, North Carolina: Duke University Press, 1927).

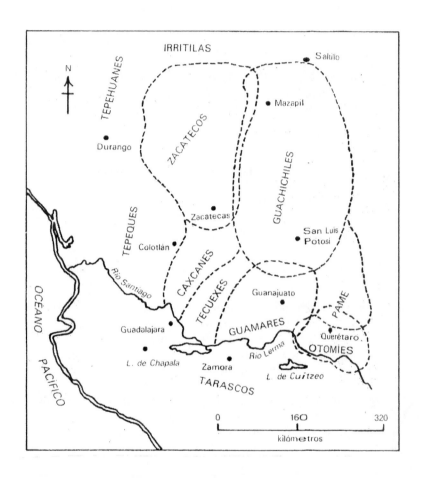

Map of Chichimeca Nations, 1550

THE INDIANS OF MEXICO

In describing this phenomenon, Mr. Powell noted that the "Indians formed the bulk of the fighting forces against the Chichimeca warriors." Continuing with this reflection, Mr. Powell wrote:

> As fighters, as burden bearers, as interpreters, as scouts, as emissaries, the pacified natives of New Spain played significant and often indispensable roles in subjugating and civilizing the Chichimeca country. Occasionally armies composed exclusively of these native warriors (particularly the Otomíes) roamed the *tierra de guerra* to seek out, defeat, and help Christianize the hostile nomad of the north. On some parts of the frontier defense against Chichimeca attacks was at times exclusively in the hands of the native population...

> Spanish authority and personnel were in most cases supervising agents for manpower supplied by Indian allies. The white men were the organizers of the effort; native allies did much of the hard work and often bore the brunt of the fighting. In the early years of the war the Spaniards placed heavy reliance upon those natives who had been wholly or partly subdued by the Cortesian conquest – Mexicans, Tarascans, Otomíes, among others.

> This use of native allies... led eventually to a virtual disappearance of the nomadic tribes as they were absorbed into the northward-moving Tarascans, Aztecs, Cholultecans, Otomíes, Tlaxcalans, Cazcanes, and others... within a few decades of the general pacification at the end of the century the Guachichiles, Zacatecos, Guamares, and other tribes or nations were disappearing as distinguishable entities in the *Gran Chichimeca*.

By the second decade of the Seventeenth Century, Mr. Powell concludes, *"the Sixteenth-Century land of war thus became fully Mexican in its mixture."* In the final analysis, we have come to realize that the history of Mexico is not the history of one people, but of many peoples. The Spanish reliance upon their Indian allies paved the way for major population movements that transformed, displaced and integrated the pre-Hispanic Indian population of Mexico. And the Mexico of today is, in fact, a manifestation of many Indian nations, initially subdued, absorbed, and assimilated into a central Hispanic culture.

As noted above, the pacification and Christianizing of so many Indian tribes led to a rapid loss of ethnic identity for the Indians in many parts of Mexico. For this reason, parish priests, in recording the baptisms and marriages of Indians, usually employed the generic terms *indio* (implying the male gender) or *india* (the female gender).

On page 103, we have reproduced the 1773 marriage record of Donna's great-great-great-great-grandparents, Jose Dionicio Delgado, an Indian, and Rita Quiteria de Lara, also an Indian. Their marriage took place in Lagos de Moreno and our translation of that document is as follows: [6]

> *In the Parish of Lagos on the 10th of July 1773, having read the marriage banns in solemn Mass on three holy days, on the 13th, 20th, and 24th of June, as required by the Holy Council of Trent, I, Father Miguel Días asked for the consent of JOSE DIONICIO DELGADO, an Indian, originally from and a resident of this parish in the post of Quarenta, legitimate son of Leon Delgado and Josefa Ramires, and RITA QUITERIA DE LARA, an Indian, originally from and a resident of this parish in Sabinda, legitimate daughter of Carlos Antonio de Lara, and of Maria Valades, and having expressed mutual consent, I married them by the present words (marriage vows)....*
> *Jose Reyes Gomes de Aguilar*
> *Miguel Diaz Sandiz*

---

[6] The marriages of 1773 for Lagos de Moreno, Jalisco are contained on Microfilm 0221516 (Salt Lake City: Genealogical Society of Utah, 1958).

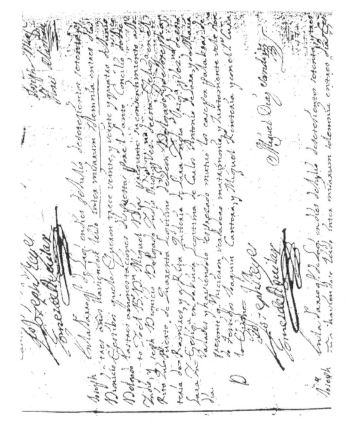

Marriage Record of Jose Dionicio Delgado and Rita Quiteria de Lara, 1773, Lagos de Moreno

Robert H. Jackson, in his very informative work *Race, Caste and Status: Indians in Colonial Spanish America*, writes that the term *indio* "became a generic term that primarily established a distinct legal and fiscal status for the indigenous population." But, according to Mr. Jackson, the ethnic label indio, as well as the other racial terms, were employed with "imprecision" by the parish priests.[7]

To illustrate the imprecision and ambiguity of the racial terms employed in the parish registers, we have reproduced another marriage record on page 105. This document, dated February 15, 1744, is the marriage record of Carlos Antonio and Maria de la Encarnacion Valades, the parents of Rita Quiteria de Lara, whose own marriage record was seen on page 103. This document is translated as follows:

> *In the Parish of Lagos on the 15th of February of 1744, having read the three marriage banns as required by the Holy Council of Trent on three holy days in Solemn Mass, and no impediments to marriage having resulted, I, Father Francisco Xavier Solis ask for the consent of CARLOS ANTONIO, a free mulato, originally from and a resident of this parish in Quarenta, legitimate son of Geronimo Disiderio, and of Nicolasa Dimas, and...*
>
> *MARIA DE LA ENCARNACION VALADES, a free mulata, originally from and a resident of the above-mentioned parish in Sabinda, legitimate daughter of Alonso Valades and of Josefa de la Pena, and both having expressed mutual (consent), I married and veiled them by the words of the present (marriage vows), that are true marriage, the witnesses present: Joachin Cervantes and Julia Padilla. They received the blessed nuptials, and with him, the priest, I signed it.*
> *Francisco Xavier Solis*

---

[7] Robert H. Jackson, *op. cit.*, pp. 4-5.

**Marriage of Carlos Antonio & Maria Valades, 1774,
Lagos de Moreno**

THE INDIANS OF MEXICO

The significance of this document is that the parish priest has classified the parents of the Indian girl, Rita Quiteria de Lara, as mulatos. The ambiguity in racial terms used by parish priests thus may have been the result of varying perceptions by different priests with varying educational and cultural backgrounds.

The comparison of the two documents brings to light another problem with the documents of mixed-race individuals in Mexico. In 1744, when Carlos Antonio was married, he had no surname. But in the 1773 document, his daughter states that his surname is de Lara. From the Sixteenth through the Nineteenth Centuries, some Indian families may have changed their surnames over a period of one or two generations.

Although the generic term *indio* was widely used in parish registers throughout Mexico, there were some areas of Mexico – as now – where the cultural indigenous identity remained strong. The closer the settlements were to the frontier regions of Mexico, the greater the likelihood of locating baptism and marriages of Indians who were, indeed, classified by their ethnic identity. In the Seventeenth and Eighteenth Centuries, the baptism and marriage registers in Hermosillo and Alamos, Sonora, included references to *Indios de Yaqui* (Yaqui Indians) or *Indios de Mayo* (Mayo Indians). Similarly, the parish registers in the northern state of Chihuahua make frequent references to Tarahumara, Apache, Concho and Yaqui Indians.

The City of Chihuahua is the capital of the state of Chihuahua. The parish registers of this city, as extracted from the Archive of the Diocese of Chihuahua, range from 1709 to 1957 and are contained on 41 rolls of microfilm. Originally copied by the Genealogical Society of Utah in 1957, these church books offer a fascinating window to the past. On page 107, we have reproduced a marriage record from these church registers.[8]

---

[8] The marriage records for the City of Chihuahua for the year 1750 are contained on Microfilm #162689 (Salt Lake City: Genealogical Society of Utah, 1957).

1750 Marriage Record of Two Apache Indians–Chihuahua

The notes in the margin of this marriage record state "Assensio de la Cruz con Getrudis Guadalupe, Yndios Apachis Viuda," which – translated into English – means "Assensio de la Cruz with Getrudis Guadalupe, Apache Indians, widow." The document is translated as follows:

> *On the 28th of December of 1750, as my lieutenant (assistant), Father Jose Ruis de Mexas, my lieutenant, having presided over everything that is right, and finding no impediments to marriage resulting, married in the face of the church, ASSENSIO DE LA CRUZ, an Apache Indian, servant of Jose Soto, with GETRUDIS GUADALUPE, an Apache Indian, widow of Francisco Miguel. Their sponsors: Lasaro de Jesus and Maria Manuela Pantoja. Witnesses: Jose Manuel and Pablo de la Cruz, and in witness thereof, I signed it.*
> *Thomas A. Jittorica*

On page 109, we have reproduced the 1751 marriage record of two Yaqui Indians, also performed at the parish church in the city of Chihuahua. The translation of this document is as follows: [9]

> *On the 12th of May of 1751, Father Jose Ruis de Mexa, my lieutenant (assistant), having resided over everything that is right, and of which finding no impediments to marriage resulting, married in the face of the church, BALTHASAR, a Yaqui Indian from the Pueblo of Saguaripa,*
>
> *With MARIA ROSALIA of the Pueblo of Torimp. Patrons: Blas and Maria, both Yaqui Indians; witnesses: Mariano Porras and Julian Villalba, and in witness thereof, I signed it.*
> *Thomas A. Jittorica*

---

[9] The marriage records for the City of Chihuahua for the year 1751 are contained on Microfilm #162689 (Salt Lake City: Genealogical Society of Utah, 1957).

1751 Marriage Record of Two Yaqui Indians-Chihuahua

The significance of this document is that it shows that the two participants were Yaqui Indians from specific pueblos. The Yaqui Indians were not indigenous to the area surrounding the City of Chihuahua. They were primarily from the coastal states of Sinaloa and Sonora. Both Balthasar and Maria Rosalia state that they are from pueblos that are located in the present-day state of Sonora. Baptism documents in some Mexican church records are also likely to show the place of origin for both parents.

On page 111, we have reproduced the 1801 baptism of an Apache Indian child at San Antonio de la Ysleta, a small mission church along the border of what is now Chihuahua and Texas.[10]

> *On the 12th of January of 1801, I, Father Rafael Benavidez, sacramental minister in this mission of San Antonio de la Ysleta, baptized solemnly and poured the holy oils on Jose Deonizo, servant in the house of Don Francisco Carbajal, of the Apache Nation. His godfather was Lieutenant Ignacio Carrasco, of whom I advised of his obligation and spiritual parentage and in witness of, I signed it.*
> *Father Rafael Benavidez*

On page 112, we have reprinted a page from the margin of the marriage register of San Fernando Cathedral in San Antonio, Texas. This page features the marriages of several couples, all of whom had an affiliation with an Indian nation. During the 1700s, some 150 different Indian groups, speaking various languages and dialects, were represented in the parish registers of the San Antonio.[11]

In the first entry, you can see that Cayetano Chualaca of the *Nacion Pasalat* married Augustina, a member of the *Nacion Patalca*. In the second entry, Buenavenuto of the *Nacion Tacame* was married to Maria

---

[10] The baptisms for Our Lady of Mt. Carmel Church in Ysleta, Texas start in 1772 and continue to 1940. This entire collection is contained on Family History Library Microfilm #0025530. This microfilm was published by the Golightly Company in 1956.

[11] The deaths and marriages of Indians at San Fernando Mission in San Antonio were microfilmed in 1957 by the Golightly Company in 1957. They are contained on Microfilm #0025438.

**1801 Baptism of Jose Dionico, Apache Indian,
San Antonio Ysleta**

**Three Indian Marriages, San Fernando Cathedral
San Antonio, Texas (1745)**

Antonia of the *Nacion Chayopina*. Finally, in the third entry, a man named Silbestre, also of the *Nacion Tacame,* was married to Theresa of the same nation (*de la misma nacion*).

In concluding this chapter, we want to stress that a genealogical investigation into your Mexican ancestry can be a very revealing experience. It is hard to predict the outcome for any one person, but we can promise that, if you persist, your understanding of your ethnic heritage is likely to be enhanced. And, as you progress backwards in time, it is possible that you will find that your own origins, like those of the nation of Mexico, are both diverse and multidimensional.

Chapter 10
In the Service of Their Country
Donna Morales

I have known John for many years and, in the course of our friendship, I have made a point of telling him about my family's patriotism. On several occasions, I told John, "My family is very patriotic. We love this country." John would usually smile and say, "That's great, Donna. My family is very patriotic too." But I would stress the fact that my Uncle Louis Dominguez had died fighting the Germans in World War II and that my family had made sacrifices for this country that we love.

One day back in 1999, John told me that he wanted to see just how patriotic my family was. He suggested that we try to get information about the details of my family's military service. It didn't take long before our friend Carole Turner (in Kansas City) located the April 25, 1945 *Kansas City Star* article reporting that my two uncles had been casualties in the last months of World War II. (The European Theater of the war ended on May 8, 1945 with the surrender of Germany – V.E. Day.)

The article reporting that the Germans had captured my uncle Erminio Dominguez and Uncle Louis had been killed in action is reproduced on page 116. Using this as an example, we want to stress that utilizing the newspaper archives in your local library may be a useful way of finding out about the military service of your family.

But, we did not stop there. John wrote to the Maryland National Archives office, from which he received a POW Report for Uncle Erminio. The Third Rangers, which Erminio had originally joined in 1942, were nearly wiped out at Cisterna, a small town located about 15 miles northeast of Anzio, in the Italian campaign of early 1944. As a result of this bloodbath, the Third Rangers were disbanded and the survivors, including Uncle Erminio, were transferred to other units.

Army and Navy Official Reports

BROTHERS ARE CASUALTIES.

Louis Dominguez Is Killed—Erminio Dominguez a Prisoner.

Cpl. Louis Dominguez, 18-year-old infantryman, was killed in action in Germany, March 21, it has been learned by his brothers and sisters. His parents are dead.

Corporal Dominguez was graduated from the Turner, Kas., grade school and entered service in August of last year. He went overseas in January.

Louis Dominguez.

A brother, Pfc. Erminio Dominguez, 22, just had been announced a prisoner of the Germans. He went into the army in 1942 and was sent overseas a year ago to the 3d U. S. Rangers.

Corporal Dominguez is survived also by two other brothers, Paul Dominguez, Turner, and Jess Dominguez, 1043 South Twenty-fourth street, Kansas City, Kansas, and two sisters, Mrs. Felica Morales, 1047 South Twenty-sixth street, and Miss Effie Dominguez, Turner.

Erminio Dominguez.

Carter, jr., son of the publisher of the Fort Worth, Tex., Star-Telegram, was safe, although a prisoner, when Swanson last saw him about January 30.

The Germans were attempting to move back inmates of Oflag 64, prison camp in the Polish corridor, ahead of the advancing Russians, Swanson said.

"Two groups of about 100 each were taken out by train, and Amon may have been with one of them," he added, "but I think he was in the group that was marching. I understand they were taken to the Luckenwalde camp about twenty miles south of Berlin."

Lieutenant Carter, an artillery officer, was captured in Africa.

U. S. GROUPS LEAVE PARIS.

Representatives and Senators to Horror Camps by Plane.

PARIS, April 24.(AP)—A group of United States senators and representatives planning to investigate German prison camp atrocities left Paris by plane today for Germany.

Members of the group which arrived in France by plane yesterday include Representative Dewey Short of Missouri, Republican.

General Eisenhower had urged that members of Congress make an inspection of German prison camps.

R. M. SANFORD DIES.

ST. LOUIS, April 24.(AP)—Robert M. Sanford, manufacturing superintendent of the Monsanto Chemical company's plant at Monsanto, Ill., died today of heart disease. He was 56.

The Capture of Erminio Dominguez/Louis Dominguez is Killed in Action-*Kansas City Star*, April 25, 1945

Uncle Erminio was then transferred to the 117th Mechanized Division (Cavalry), which took part in the invasion of Southern France in August 1944. As indicated by the POW Report, reproduced on page 118, Erminio Dominguez, a private in the 117th Mechanized and a native of Kansas, was reported as captured in France on September 2, 1944. Towards the bottom of the page, you will see the listing *Camp*. It is through this document that we learned that Uncle Erminio was detained in *Stalag 7A* near Moosburg, Bavaria. He was released from the POW camp eight months after his capture.

While my Uncle Erminio was alive, he was very humble and modest about his wartime record. I never knew that he had been a highly decorated soldier and that he had received four bronze stars, the Purple Heart, service ribbon and a good conduct medal. However, last year, we consulted the Kansas City Public Library and found Uncle Erminio's obituary. The obituary, appearing in the *Kansas City Star* on June 10, 1996, reads in part as follows:

> Erminio L. Dominguez, 74, Kansas City, KS, died June 8, 1996, at his home.... Mr. Dominguez was born in Kansas City, KS, and was a lifelong area resident. He was a former forklift operator for the Santa Fe Railroad for 45 years, before retiring in 1986. He was a member of the First Spanish American Baptist Church of Merriam, KS. Mr. Dominguez served in the U.S. Army during WWII. He saw combat action in France and Italy. He was captured and spent eight months as a prisoner of war. He was given four bronze stars, Purple Heart, service ribbon and a good conduct medal. He was a member of the V.F.W. in Kansas City, Mo. On February 15, 1947, Erminio was united in marriage to Carmen Garcia Dominguez, who survives of the home...

The obituary also gave Erminio's next of kin and other information. As can readily be recognized, the obituary of a veteran may be useful in obtaining additional information about the veteran's life. Such obituaries can be located through public libraries or from genealogical websites such as *Ancestry.com*.

WWII POW Report

Serial Number: 37248014

Name: DOMINGUEZ ERMINIO I

Grade alpha: PVT *Private*

Grade Code: 8 *Private*

Service Code: 1 *Army*

Arm of Service: CAV

Arm of Service Code: 93

Date Reported (DDMMY): 02094 *02 September 1944*

Race: 1 *White*

State of Residence: 73 *Kansas*

Type of Organization: 267

Parent Unit Number: 0117

Parent Unit Type: 08

Area: 76 *France*

Latest Report (DDMMY): 24075 *24 July 1945*

Source of Report: 1 *Official*

Status: 8 *Returned to military control, liberated, or repatriated*

Detaining Power: 1 *Germany*

Camp: 013 *Stalag 7A Moosburg, Bavaria* 48-12

Four numbers separated by a "-" indicate camp's latitude and longitude

Repatriation Status: *Meaning unknown except in the case of Deceased American POWs, Pacific Theater, who died in ship sinkings, 1944. Repatriation Status and Ship Sinking fields are combined to indicate a particular ship.*

Ship Sinking:

The above report is from a database application that the Center for Electronic Records developed to extract and print individual records from World War II Prisoners of War Punchcards, [Electronic Records]; Records of the Office of the Provost Marshal General, RG 389, National Archives at College Park.

The report has three parts: the field name (in bold letters on gray background), the data as recorded in the electronic datafile, and where the recorded data is in code form, the meaning of the relevant code in italics.

POW Report, Erminio Dominguez

If your relative was one of the 405,399 American military personnel who lost his life during World War II, you may want to visit the *American Battle Monuments Commission for World War II* website. This online memorial pays tribute to the 78,976 *missing in action* and the 93,242 soldiers who were *killed in action* and subsequently buried at cemeteries overseas. Because my Uncle Louis was buried at one of these cemeteries, we were able to obtain a copy of his lovely memorial, which has been reproduced on page 120.

The *American Battle Monuments Commission for World War II* can be accessed at *http://www.americanwardead.com/searchww.htm*. If you have a desire to locate military records of World War II veterans in your family, you may want to write to the following address:

National Personnel Records
9700 Page Blvd
St. Louis MO 63132

Their website can be accessed at:
http://www.nara.gov/regional/stlouis.html. A useful NARA site entitled "Frequently Asked Questions (FAQ)" can be accessed at *http://www.nara.gov/regional/mprfaq.html.* And still another helpful site (*Military Records of World War II Veterans*) will be found at the following URL: *http://www.ibiblio.org/hyperwar/USN/USN-ref.html*

When World War II started, my father immediately decided that he must serve his country in its time of need. However, my mother, with a couple of small children to take care, did not share his enthusiasm and stopped him from enlisting. As it turns out, my father stayed at home and helped lend moral and spiritual support to my mother's family during their darkest days after the capture of Uncle Erminio and the death of Uncle Louis. Nevertheless, my father was required by law to register at the local draft board and, on page 121, you can see his *Draft Registration*. This type of document can be obtained from:

The Records Division
Selective Service National Headquarters
Arlington, VA 22209-4047

AMERICAN BATTLE MONUMENTS COMMISSION

THE WORLD WAR II HONOR ROLL

Louis Dominguez

Private First Class, U.S. Army

37749907

289th Infantry Regiment, 75th Infantry Division

Entered the Service from: Missouri
Died: March 31, 1945
Buried at: Plot G Row 21 Grave 21
Netherlands American Cemetery
Margraten, Netherlands

Awards: Purple Heart

**Tribute to Louis Dominguez (KIA)-American Battle
Monuments Commission (World War II)**

Draft Registration, Daniel Morales

If you are trying to do research on the tremendous contributions of Hispanic Americans to America's military, you may want to purchase *Hispanics in America's Defense* (Paperback reprint edition, August 1997), which is available through *Amazon.com*. This work, originally published by the Office of the Deputy Assistant Secretary of Defense for Military Manpower and Personnel Policy, pays a wonderful tribute to the participation of Hispanic-Americans in all the American wars and describes the acts of valor that earned medals for many of them.[1]

In putting together a family history, telling the story of your family's military history is an important ingredient. When we tell the story about Mexican Americans who have served our country in wartime, we are paying tribute to the sacrifices that they made for our freedom.

---

[1] *Hispanics in America's Defense* (Collingdale, Pennsylvania: Diane Publishing Co. 1997).

Chapter 11
Getting Prepared
John Schmal

It is time for you to prepare the paperwork on your own family. The best method of organizing all your information for a visit to the Family History Center in your neighborhood or to meet with your relatives is to put your information on a pedigree chart.

On the following page, you will see Donna's pedigree chart, extending back five generations to her great-great-great-grandparents. Then, on page 125, we have reproduced a second pedigree chart that starts with Donna's great-great-grandfather, Jose Casimiro Morales, and goes back another five generations. These charts employ the following fields:

1. B. (Born) – When was this person born?
2. P. (Place) – Where was this person born?
3. M. (Married) – When was this person married?
4. P. (Place) – Where was this person married?
5. D. (Died) – When did this person die?
6. P. (Place) – Where did this person die?

Every pedigree chart starts with a given person. All other people listed on the chart are direct ancestors of that person (not siblings, aunts or uncles). To determine the parents of a given person, you merely take the corresponding number of the person you are concerned with and double it, to find the father, and add one, to find the mother.

If you are seeking the parents of Geronimo Dominguez on the following page, you will need to find his corresponding number first. Once you have determined that his number is 6, you will look for his parents at numbers 12 (his father) and 13 (his mother).

On the last page of this section, we shall include an Ancestry Chart, published by Everton Publishers and used extensively by most of the Family History Centers. However, starting on this page, we have created a Mexican-American Genealogical Research Outline to help you get started.

Pedigree Chart

Pedigree Chart of Donna Morales

Pedigree Chart

2 Jose Nosiforo Morales
B: 10 Aug 1755
P: Lagos de Moreno
M: 8 Feb 1794
P: Lagos de Moreno
D:
P:

1 Jose Casimiro Morales
B: 12 Mar 1804
P: Moreno de los Lagos
M: 26 Jun 1836
P: Ojuelos, Jalisco
D:
P:

Zeferina Valades
(Spouse of no. 1)

3 Maria Josefa Delgado
B: 7 Apr 1776
P: Lagos de Moreno
D:
P:

4 Francisco Xavier Morales
B: 23 Feb 1725
P: Lagos de Moreno
M: 4 Nov 1754
P: Lagos de Moreno
D:
P:

5 Lucrecia R Montelongo
B: 9 May 1735
P: Lagos de Moreno
D:
P:

6 Jose Dionisio Delgado
B:
P:
M: 10 Jul 1773
P: Lagos de Moreno
D:
P:

7 Rita Quiteria de Lara
B:
P:
D:
P:

8 Juan Morales
B: 24 Jun 1698
P: Lagos de Moreno
M: 15 Feb 1722
P: Lagos de Moreno
D:
P:

9 Paula Petrona de la Cruz
B: 19 Jul 1705
P: Lagos de Moreno
D:
P:

10 Toribio Montelongo
B: 22 Apr 1706
P: Lagos de Moreno
M: 20 Feb 1730
P: Lagos de Moreno
D:
P:

11 Mariana Gomes
B: 15 Jul 1703
P: Lagos de Moreno
D:
P:

12 Jose Leonicio Delgado
B: 25 Apr 1723
P: Lagos de Moreno
M: 20 Sep 1745
P: Lagos de Moreno
D:
P:

13 Josefa Ramirez Torres
B: 17 May 1722
P: Lagos de Moreno
D:
P:

14 Carlos Antonio Lopes
B: 11 Nov 1725
P: Lagos de Moreno
M: 15 Feb 1741
P: Lagos de Moreno
D:
P:

15 Maria F Valades
B:
P:
D:
P:

16 Miguel Morales
B:
M:
D:

17 Maria de la Cruz
B:
D:

18 Martin de la Cruz
B:
M:
D:

19 Silveria Ortega
B:
D:

20 Pedro Montelongo
B:
M: 16 Jan 1692
D:

21 Pascuala Espirito Torres
B:
D:

22 Alexo Gomes
B:
M: 5 Mar 1696
D:

23 Natiana Ortiz Ramirez
B:
D:

24 Juan Delgado
B: 10 Feb 1694
M: 12 Nov 1716
D:

25 Felipa de Vega
B:
D:

26 Diego Santiago
B:
M: 21 Jul 1715
D:

27 Maria Gertrudis Torres
B:
D:

28 Geronimo D de la Cruz
B: 21 May 1702
M: 19 Nov 1724
D:

29 Nicolasa Dimas
B:
D:

30 Alonso Valades
B:
M: 30 Oct 1721
D:

31 Josefa de la Pena
B:
D:

32
33
34
35
36
37
38
39
40
41

42 Lazaro Torres
43 Margarita Rivera

44

45

46 Jose Ortis
47 Tomasina Ramirez
48 Juan Delgado
49 Juana de Campos

50
51
52
53

54 Nicolas de Torres
55 Pasquala Garcia
56 Juan Lopez
57 Maria de la Ascencion

58
59

60 Alonso Valades
61 Gertrudis de Salazar

62

63

Prepared by
John P. Schmal

Telephone Date prepared
24 Feb 2001

Pedigiree Chart of Jose Casimiro Morales

125

MEXICAN-AMERICAN
GENEALOGICAL RESEARCH OUTLINE

1. STARTING OUT -- SOURCES OF INFORMATION
    A. Collect information from family members. Questions to ask:
        1. Dates of birth, marriage, places where ancestors lived.
        2. Where did our ancestors live in 1920 (for the 1920 census)?
        3. Did our ancestors become citizens? (Naturalization records).
        4. Did we have non-citizen immigrant ancestors living in the United States in 1940-44? (Alien Registration forms).
        5. Do we have passports or visas for our ancestors? (Using such numbers, we can get additional info from the INS.)
    B. Birth, marriage, death certificates (civil or church).
        1. Find vital records on county or state level.
        http://www.surnameguide.com/vital_records/vitalrecords.htm
            http://vitalrec.com/usmap.html
            http://www.cyndislist.com/usvital.htm
    C. If available, obtain naturalization records.
        1. Visit the National Archives site:
            http://www.archives.gov/facilities/index.html
            http://www.archives.gov/research_room/genealogy/
            immigrant_arrivals/mexican_border_crossing.html
    D. Utilizing the Freedom of Information Act, locate Alien Registration Forms or visas. Write to:
        1. INS Freedom of Information
            2nd Floor, ULLB, 425 I Street, NW Washington, D.C. 20536
        2. Consult INS websites:
            http://www.ins.usdoj.gov/graphics/fieldoffices/about
            us.htm
            http://www.ins.usdoj.gov/graphics/aboutins/history/
            tools.html

      E. Border-crossing records:
          1.   See National Archives site for published microfilm sources:
              http://www.archives.gov/research_room/genealogy/immigrant_arrivals/mexican_bordre_crossing.html
          2.   Write to the National Archives for documents.
      F. Obtain Obituaries, Cemetery records, and Funeral Records by consulting newspapers, local libraries, historical societies, genealogical societies and funeral homes

2.   CREATE A PEDIGREE CHART TO UNDERSTAND FAMILIAL RELATIONSHIPS.

3.   LOCATION ANALYSIS (Once you have found out what municipio, hacienda, or city your family came from in Mexico):
      A. Purchase a large-scale map of your ancestral region. Such maps are available through Amazon.com or can be purchased at map stores.
      B.   Locate your ancestral town on a large-scale map.
          1.   Which municipio is the town in?
          2.   What church did they attend? (Remember that church records and civil records may be in different locations).
          3.   Is the town near the boundary of another? jurisdiction (municipio, estado)?
          4.   If your ancestral town was a small hacienda and cannot be found on maps, locate the geographic coordinates in a Gazetteer of Mexico, then go to a large-scale map and note the municipio in which it lies.
      C.   Search for the town or municipio in the Family History Catalog:
http://www.familysearch.org/Eng/Library/FHLC/frameset_fhlc.asp
          1.   Civil records (at the municipio level).
          2.   Church records (Parish or Diocese)
          3.   Other (census, padrones, military, family histories).

      D.   Search the International Genealogical Index (IGI).
 http://www.familysearch.org/Eng/Search/frameset_search.asp
      E.   Write to the Catholic Archdiocese office for records.
         1. Consult:
http://home.att.net/~Local_Catholic/Catholic-Mexico.htm
      F.   Write to the State Civil Registers for records:
http://www.gksoft.com/govt/en/mx.html

4.   DOCUMENT INTERPRETATION
      A.   Problems in translating old documents:
         1. Abbreviations are common in older records.
         2. Surnames in Latin America went through many
            variant spellings over the centuries.
         3. Interchanging Letters and other spelling
            variations (Consult Spanish Records
            Extraction, pp. 3-12 and 3-13.)
         4. Handwriting
      B.   Consult publications that explain how to interpret
         documents:
         1.   George R. Ryskamp, "*Finding Your Hispanic
            Roots*," 264 pages, available from SHHAR.
         2.   "*Spanish Records Extraction Manual*," 126 pages,
            available from SHHAR.

5.   PUTTING IT ALL TOGETHER
      A.   Network with other researchers on the Internet.
      B.   Look for government and municipio sites to learn
         more about the area:
      C. Post queries on the Mexico Genweb:
         http://www.rootsweb.com/~mexwgw/
      D. Consult Cyndi's List:
         http://www.cyndislist.com/hispanic.htm
      E.   Understanding the historical perspective. It is important
         to understand the history of the area.
         1.   War, oppression, poverty and civil unrest cause
            people to move around.
         2.   Tourist information may contain some historical
            info.

3.   Consult the "Los Municipios" series for each Mexican state for a description of each municipio.

F.   Tell a story about your family by integrating the history of the area with the history of the family.

Warning: An important word of warning for beginners. Large amounts of genealogical data appear on many sites in the Internet. However, information on the Internet may be faulty or incorrect. Dates of birth or marriage given on a website may be false. The only real way you can prove your ancestry is through DOCUMENT VERIFICATION.

A true researcher will find the church or civil documents, either through his or her own efforts, or those of another family member. You will never be certain of your information until the documents are verified.

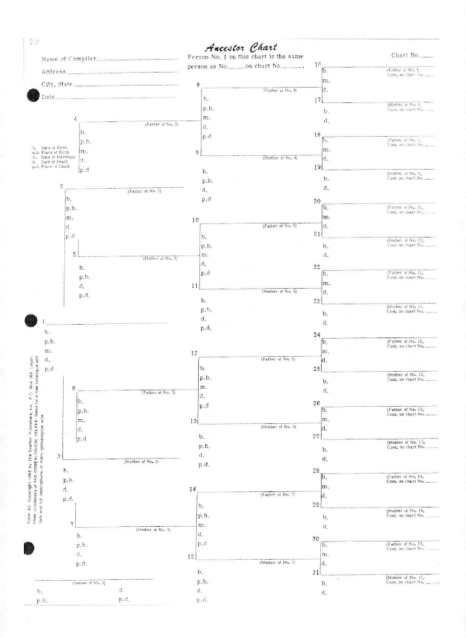

Bibliography

American Battle Monuments Commission. The World War II Honor Roll. <http://www.americanwardead.com/searchww.htm>. May 20, 2001.

Archivo General de Indias. *Catalogo de Pasajeros a Indias - Siglos XVI, XVII y XVIII, Volumen 1 (1509-1534).* Sevilla, Spain.

Clancy, Patrick. Military Records of World War II Veterans. Online: <http://www.ibiblio.org/hyperwar/USN/USN-ref.html>. June 3, 2001.

Cross, Harry E. and Sandos, James A. *Across the Border: Rural Development in Mexico and Recent Migration to the United States.* Berkeley, California: Institute of Governmental Studies, University of California, Berkeley, 1981.

Davies, Nigel. *The Ancient Kingdoms of Mexico.* London: Penguin Books, 1990.

Department of Defense. *The Hispanics in America's Defense.* Collingdale, Pennsylvania: Diane Publishing Co., 1997.

Gerhard, Peter. *The Northern Frontier of New Spain.* Princeton, New Jersey: Princeton University Press, 1982.

Grimes, Barbara F. (ed.). "Ethnologue: Languages of the World" (14th edition). Dallas, Texas: SIL International, 2001.

Gutiérrez, David G. (ed.). *Between Two Worlds: Mexican Immigrants in the United States.* Wilmington, Delaware: Scholarly Resources, 1996.

Immigration and Naturalization Service. Historical Research Tools. Online: <http://www.ins.usdoj.gov/graphics/aboutins/history/Tools.html>. June 3, 2001.

BIBLIOGRAPHY

Family History Library. *Spanish Records Extraction*. Salt Lake City, Utah: Family History Library, 1986.

Intellectual Reserve, The Family History Library Catalog. Online <http://familysearch.com/Search/searchcatalog.asp>. June 2, 2001.

Jackson, Robert H. *Race, Caste, and Status: Indians in Colonial Spanish America*. Albuquerque, New Mexico: University of New Mexico Press, 1999.

Jennings, Francis. *The Founders of America: How Indians Discovered The Land, Pioneered in it, and Created Great Classical Civilizations, How They Were Plunged Into a Dark Age by Invasion and Conquest, and How They Are Reviving* New York: W. W. Norton & Company, Inc., 1993.

Jiménez, Carlos M. *The Mexican American Heritage*. Berkeley, California: TQS Publications, 1994 (2nd edition).

Kansas Ethnic Council. *The Ethnic History of Wyandotte County*. Kansas City: Kansas Ethnic Council, 1992.

Marks, Richard Lee. *Cortés: The Great Adventurer and the Fate of Aztec Mexico*. New York: Alfred A. Knopf, 1994.

Mason, J. Alden. "The Native Languages of Middle America" in *The Maya and Their Neighbors*. New York: Appleton-Century Company, 1940.

McDowell, Jack (ed.). *Mexico*. Menlo Park, California: Lane Magazine & Book Company, 1973.

McWilliams, Carey. *North From Mexico*. New York: Greenwood Press, 1968.

Mecham, J. Lloyd. *Francisco de Ibarra and Neuva Vizcaya*. Durham, North Carolina, Duke University Press, 1927.

BIBLIOGRAPHY

Meier, Matt S. and Feliciano Rivera. *The Chicanos: A History of Mexican Americans*. New York: Hill and Wang, 1972.

Meier, Matt S. and Feliciano Ribera. *Mexican Americans, American Mexicans: From Conquistadors to Chicanos*. New York: Hill and Wang, 1993.

Meyer, Michael C. *The Course of Mexican History*. New York: Oxford University Press, 1987.

Morales, Donna S. and Schmal, John P. *My Family Through Time: The Story of a Mexican-American Family*. Los Angeles, California, 2000 (not yet published).

National Archives and Records Administration. *Mexican Border Crossing Records*. Online: <http://www.nara.gov/genealogy/immigration/mexican.html>. March 20, 2001.

Powell, Philip Wayne,. *Soldiers, Indians and Silver: North America's First Frontier War*. Tempe, Arizona: Center for Latin American Studies, Arizona State University, 1973.

Prechtel-Kluskens, Claire. "Mexican Border Crossing Records (3 parts)," *National Genealogical Society Newsletter,* Vol. 25, Nos. 3-5 (May-Oct. 1999): 156-157, 159, 182-183, 287-281.

Reisler, Mark. *By the Sweat of Their Brown: Mexican Immigrant Labor in the United States, 1900-1940*. Westport, Connecticut: Greenwood Press, 1976.

Ryskamp, George R. *Finding Your Hispanic Roots*. Baltimore, Maryland: Genealogical Publishing Co., Inc.

United States Labor Department. *Eighteenth Annual Report of the Secretary of Labor for the Fiscal Year Ended June 30, 1930.* Washington,D.C.: United States Government Printing Office, 1930.

BIBLIOGRAPHY

United States Labor Department. *Twenty-Eighth Annual Report of the Secretary of Labor for the Fiscal Year Ended June 30, 1940.* Washington,D.C.: United States Government Printing Office, 1940.

Van Young, Eric, "The Indigenous Peoples of Western Mexico From the Spanish Invasion to the Present," in Richard E.W. Adams and Murdo J. MacLeod, *The Cambridge History of the Native Peoples of the Americas: Volume II, Mesoamerica, Part 2.* Cambridge, UK: Cambridge University Press, 2000.

Wasserman, Mark. *Everyday Life and Politics in Nineteenth Century Mexico: Men, Women, and War.* Albuquerque: The University of New Mexico Press, 2000.

INDEX

INDEX

INDEX

INDEX

BIOGRAPHIES

Donna S. Morales.

Donna Morales is a native of Kansas City. Ms. Morales and Mr. Schmal have known each other for 12 years and collaborated on an unpublished book chronicling the 400-year history of Ms. Morales' family. Ms. Morales is a family research historian and is a member of the Society for Hispanic Historical and Ancestral Research (SHHAR) and Familia. She occasionally contributes article to the SHHAR newsletter, www.somosprimos.com. Ms. Morales works for an insurance company in Houston, Texas.

John P. Schmal.

John Schmal is a native of Hermosa Beach, California. He is a genealogist, with a specialty in Mexican lineages. Mr. Schmal belongs to the Association of Professional Genealogists, Familia, the Genealogy Society of Hispanic America, and the Society for Hispanic Historical and Ancestral Research (SHHAR). Mr. Schmal is the Staff Historian and Indexer for the SHHAR newsletter, www.somosprimos.com, and gives professional lectures on Mexican-American genealogy and indigenous Mexico. Mr. Schmal works for a publishing company in Chatsworth, California.